Broadway

The Longest Street in the U. S.

Keith Goldstein

—
AMERICA
—
THROUGH
—
TIME

Ａmerica Ｔhrough Ｔime®
An imprint of Ｓutton Ｐublishing Ｉnc.
www.through-time.com

First published 2025
Copyright © Keith Goldstein 2025

ISBN 978-1-63499-553-5

Typeset in 10pt on 13pt Sabon
Printed and bound in England

Introduction

Broadway is not merely a street; it is a cultural artery coursing through the heart of New York City. Stretching over 13 miles from the southern tip of Manhattan to the Bronx, Broadway stands as one of the oldest and most iconic streets in the United States. While often synonymous with the glitz and glamour of the theater district, Broadway's essence transcends its bright marquees and dramatic stages. It is a living tapestry, weaving together countless stories of individuals, each moving with their unique purpose and pace. For street photographers, Broadway is an ever-evolving canvas, teeming with life, movement, and emotion. Through their lenses, they capture the essence of this historic thoroughfare, immortalizing its people, architecture, and vibrant energy.

To understand Broadway is to delve into its dual nature: as a thoroughfare of global cultural significance and as a microcosm of daily life in New York City. Its allure is not confined to Times Square or the lights of the Great White Way. Broadway offers a fascinating interplay between history and modernity, high art and street life, and quiet moments and boisterous energy. Each block has a story to tell, making it an endless source of inspiration for street photographers and storytellers alike.

Broadway's history stretches back long before Dutch settlers arrived in the seventeenth century. Originally a Native American trail called the Wickquasgeck Road, it wound its way through the dense forests of Manhattan Island. For the Lenape people, the trail served as a crucial path for trade and communication. When the Dutch established New Amsterdam, they preserved the road's path, which eventually became Broadway. Its name, derived from the Dutch term "Breede Weg," or "Broad Way," reflects its importance as a main thoroughfare. Unlike the rigid grid system that dominates most of Manhattan, Broadway retains its original, meandering path, offering a visual reminder of its pre-colonial origins. Walking along Broadway today is akin to tracing the footsteps of centuries past, an experience that resonates deeply with history buffs and curious wanderers alike.

For street photographers, Broadway's irregularity presents a visual feast. The street's curves and deviations provide unexpected vantage points and opportunities for dramatic compositions. A photographer standing at the intersection of Broadway and Canal Street, for instance, can capture the convergence of angles, buildings, and human activity in a way that feels uniquely organic compared to the geometric precision of other New York streets.

Street photography is about storytelling, and Broadway offers an endless array of stories to tell. From its southern terminus in the Financial District to its northern reaches in the Bronx, Broadway traverses a wide spectrum of neighborhoods, each with its distinct character. This variety is what makes Broadway such a compelling subject for photographers. In the Financial District, the street is lined with imposing skyscrapers and historic landmarks like Trinity Church. Here, photographers often focus on contrasts: the shadow of One World Trade Center falling over the cobblestones of Wall Street, or a lone jogger passing the *Charging Bull* statue in the early morning light. The area's corporate energy, punctuated by moments of quiet introspection, reflects the dual nature of Broadway as both a place of work and reflection.

As Broadway moves northward, it cuts through neighborhoods like SoHo, with its cobblestone streets and cast-iron buildings, and Union Square, a bustling hub of commerce and protest. Each of these areas offers its own photographic opportunities. In SoHo, a photographer might capture a fashion-forward pedestrian walking past a graffiti-covered wall, while Union Square offers the spectacle of street performers, protestors, and vendors. These scenes reveal the dynamism and diversity of life along Broadway.

No exploration of Broadway would be complete without a visit to Times Square. Often referred to as "The Crossroads of the World," Times Square is synonymous with Broadway's theater district and its global cultural influence. It is a place of contrasts: overwhelming crowds and moments of individual introspection, dazzling lights and the quiet hum of humanity beneath the surface. For photographers, Times Square is both a challenge and a treasure trove. The sheer density of people and visual stimuli can feel chaotic, but within that chaos lies beauty. A street photographer might capture the determined stride of a theatergoer rushing to a matinee, the playful antics of costumed performers vying for tips, or the reflective gaze of a tourist staring up at the illuminated billboards. Each of these moments adds another layer to the story of Times Square, a place where the extraordinary becomes ordinary.

Beyond the theater marquees, Times Square is also a reflection of consumer culture and globalization. The towering advertisements, promoting everything from Broadway shows to global brands, create a surreal backdrop for candid photography. These images often juxtapose the grandiosity of the advertisements with the individuality of the people below, highlighting the tension between the collective and the personal.

Broadway's theater district is not just a place; it is an institution. Stretching from 41st to 54th Street and bounded by Sixth and Eighth Avenues, the district is home to over forty theaters, each with its unique history and character. For performers, landing a role in a Broadway production is the pinnacle of success, and for audiences, attending a Broadway show is a quintessential New York experience. Theater photographers often focus on the actors and the productions themselves, but street photographers find inspiration in the scenes outside the theaters. The anticipation of audiences lining up before a show, the jubilant crowds spilling onto the sidewalks afterward, and the quiet moments of aspiring actors rehearsing their lines in the shadow of a marquee all tell the story of Broadway as a place of dreams and ambition.

The architecture of the theaters themselves is also a draw for photographers. The ornate facades of venues like the Lyceum Theatre or the modern glass exteriors of newer establishments create a visual dialogue between tradition and innovation. Capturing these structures against the backdrop of a bustling street offers a unique perspective on Broadway's role as both a historic and contemporary cultural hub.

While Times Square and the theater district often steal the spotlight, Broadway's charm extends far beyond these areas. Heading north, the street winds through neighborhoods like the Upper West Side, Harlem, and Washington Heights, each with its own identity and atmosphere. These neighborhoods provide a glimpse into the everyday lives of New Yorkers, offering a stark contrast to the commercialized energy of midtown. In the Upper West Side, Broadway is lined with classic brownstones, boutique shops, and leafy streets. Photographers here might focus on the interplay of architecture and nature, capturing scenes of children playing in Riverside Park or the reflection of autumn leaves in shop windows. The area's quiet elegance is a reminder that Broadway is not just a place of performance but also a place of residence and community.

Harlem, with its rich cultural history, offers a different kind of energy. Here, Broadway intersects with the legacy of the Harlem Renaissance and the vibrant cultural expressions of the present day. Street musicians, community murals, and bustling markets provide a wealth of photographic opportunities. Capturing the spirit of Harlem means paying attention to the rhythms of life: the laughter of children, the calls of street vendors, and the beats of jazz spilling from a café. Further uptown in Washington Heights, Broadway becomes a celebration of immigrant culture, particularly the Dominican community. Photographers here might capture the vibrant colors of a bodega, the lively conversations of families gathered on stoops, or the joyful chaos of a parade. These images reveal a side of Broadway that is deeply rooted in the stories of the people who call it home.

Broadway is a street that never stands still. Over the centuries, it has evolved from a Native American trail to a Dutch colonial road to the bustling thoroughfare it is today. This evolution is reflected not only in its physical changes but also in its cultural significance. Broadway has witnessed the rise and fall of industries, the shifting demographics of neighborhoods, and the ever-changing landscape of art and commerce. For street photographers, this constant evolution provides endless inspiration. The juxtaposition of old and new is a recurring theme in Broadway photography. A shot of a sleek modern skyscraper rising behind a centuries-old church, or a luxury car passing a street vendor's cart, captures the duality of a street that is both rooted in history and relentlessly forward-looking.

Broadway is more than a street; it is a living, breathing embodiment of New York City's essence. It is a place where history and modernity intersect, where dreams are pursued and realized, and where the diversity of human experience is on full display. Through the eyes of street photographers, Broadway's vibrancy is captured and celebrated, revealing the intricate interplay of architecture, culture, and humanity. From the financial hustle of downtown to the cultural vibrancy of Harlem and beyond, Broadway is a journey in itself. It is a street that tells the story of New York City and its people, one image at a time. For those who walk its length, photograph its scenes, or simply marvel at its legacy, Broadway offers not just a thoroughfare but a glimpse into the soul of the city that never sleeps.

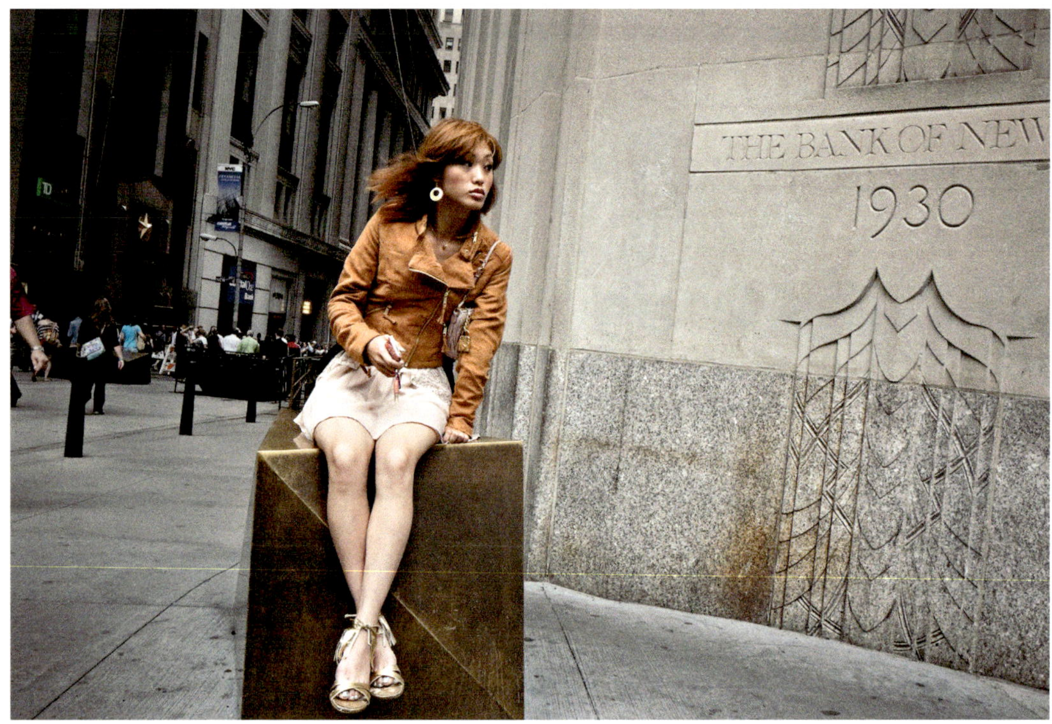

A woman waits for a friend at the corner of Broadway and Exchange Place.

Opposite page: During his shift, a nut vendor has a cigarette break.

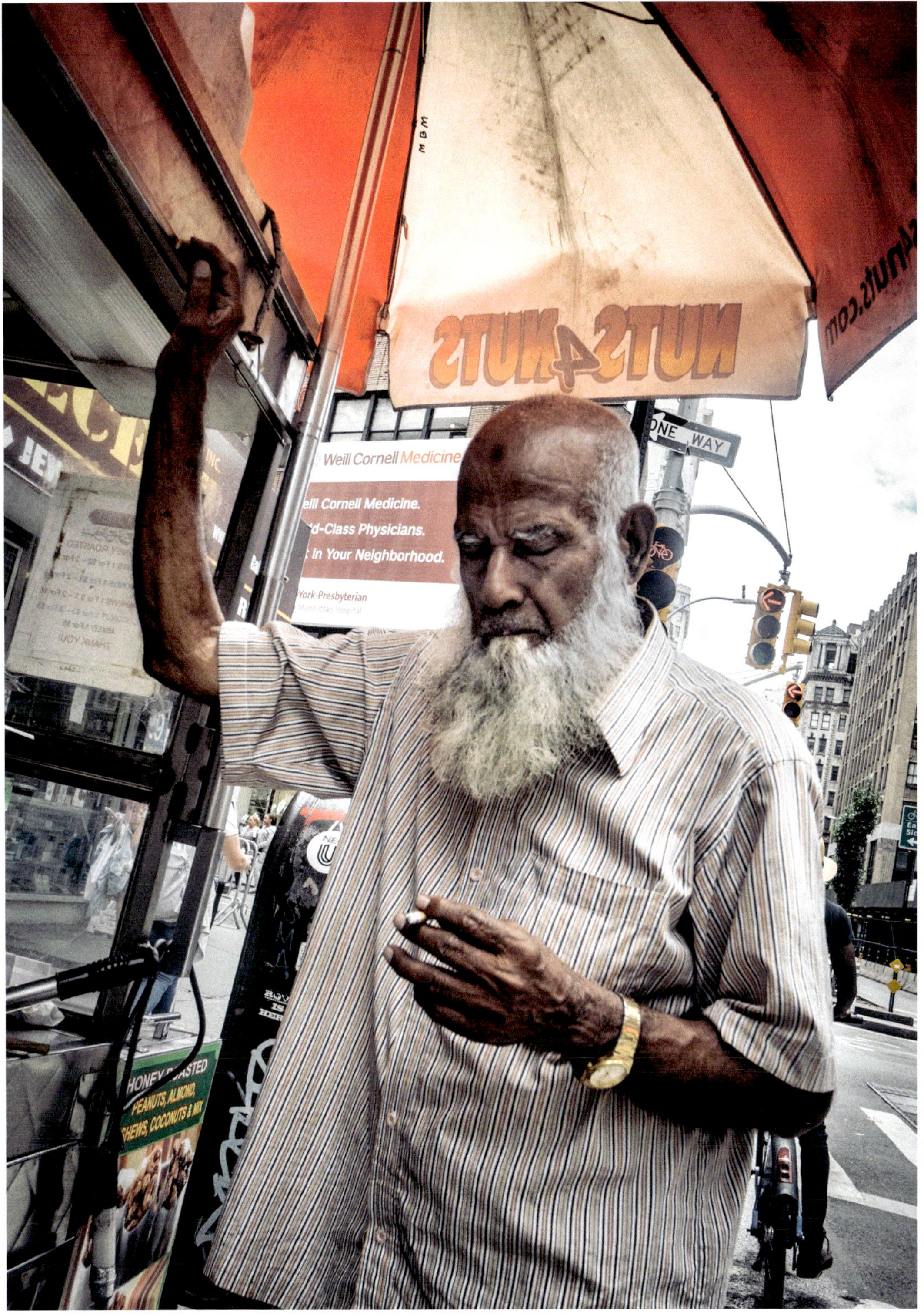

NUTS4NUTS
4nuts.com
Weill Cornell Medicine
eill Cornell Medicine.
d-Class Physicians.
t in Your Neighborhood.
York-Presbyterian
ONE WAY
HONEY ROASTED
PEANUTS, ALMOND,
HEWS, COCONUTS & MIX

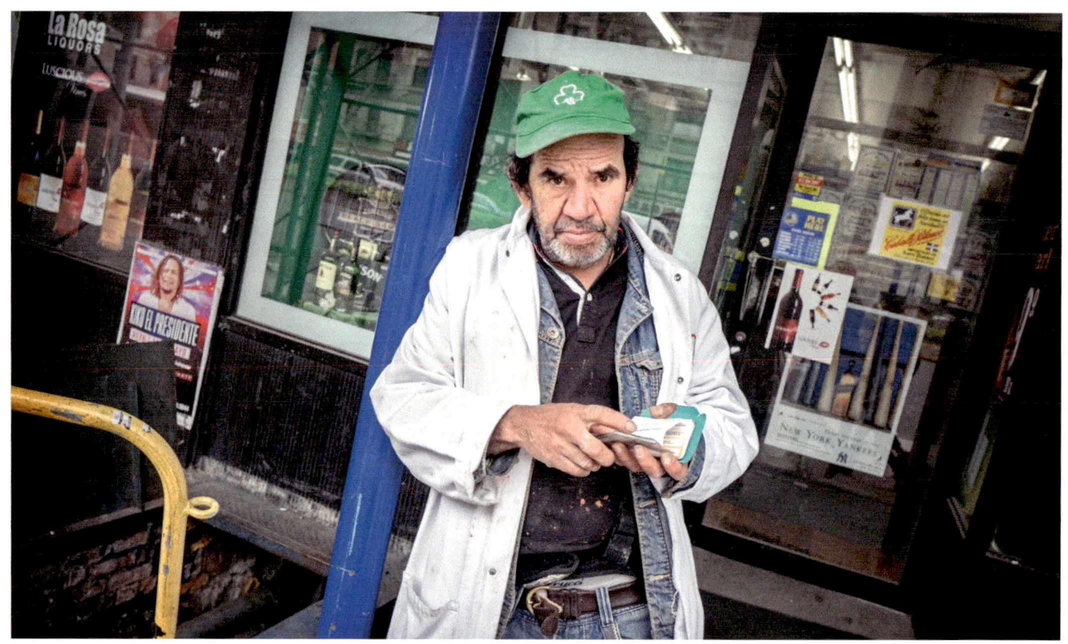

A deliveryman in front of a liquor store.

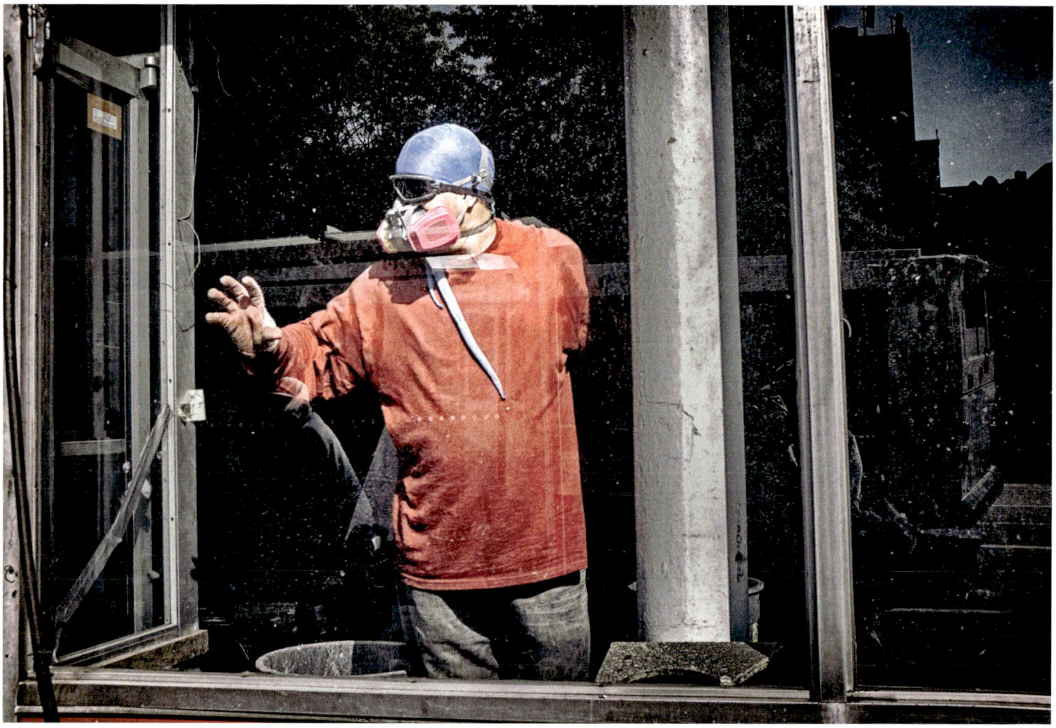

A construction worker peers out from behind a window.

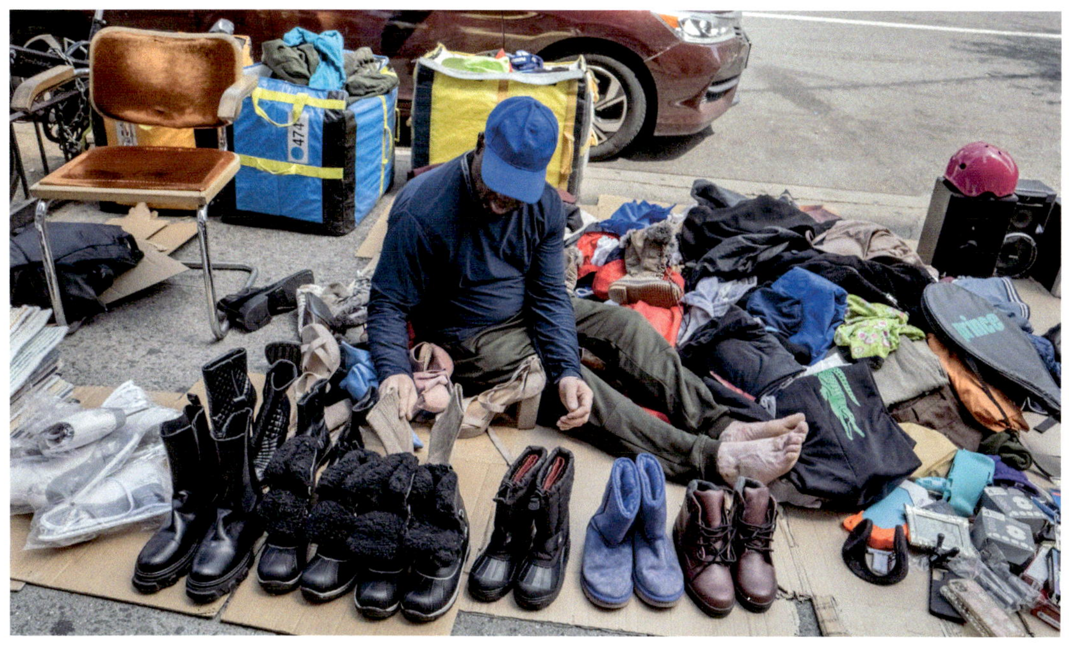

Selling shoes and other articles along Broadway.

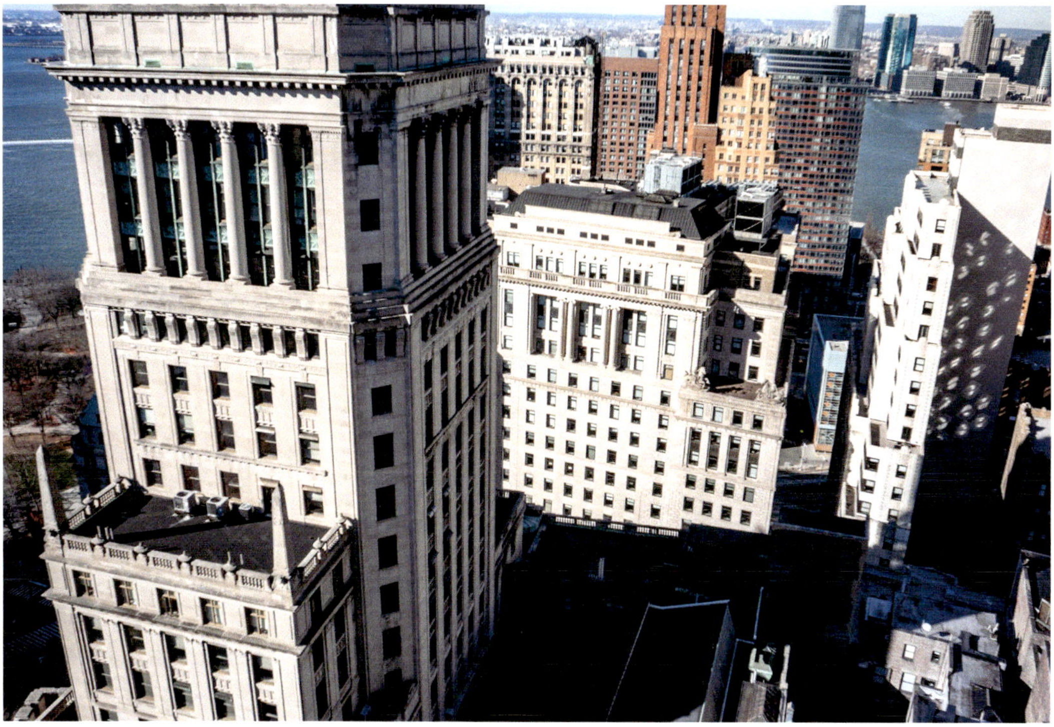

View of buildings along lower Broadway with the Standard Oil Building to the left.

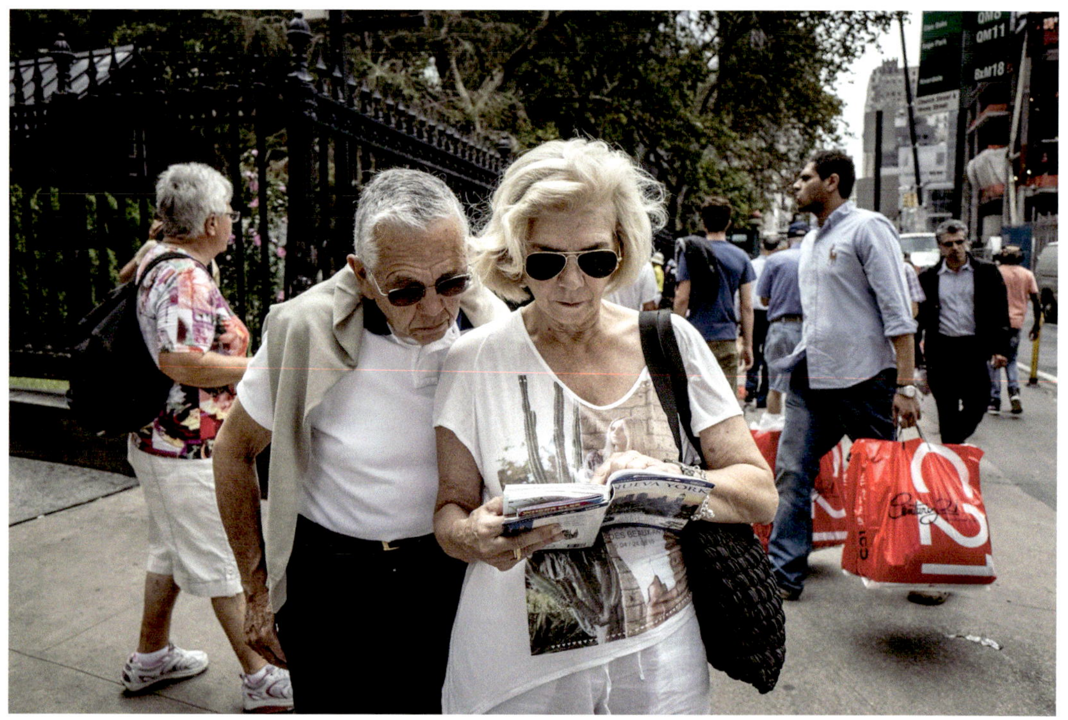

Tourists look at a NYC guidebook outside Trinity Church Cemetery.

Opposite page: A window washer in a clothing store.

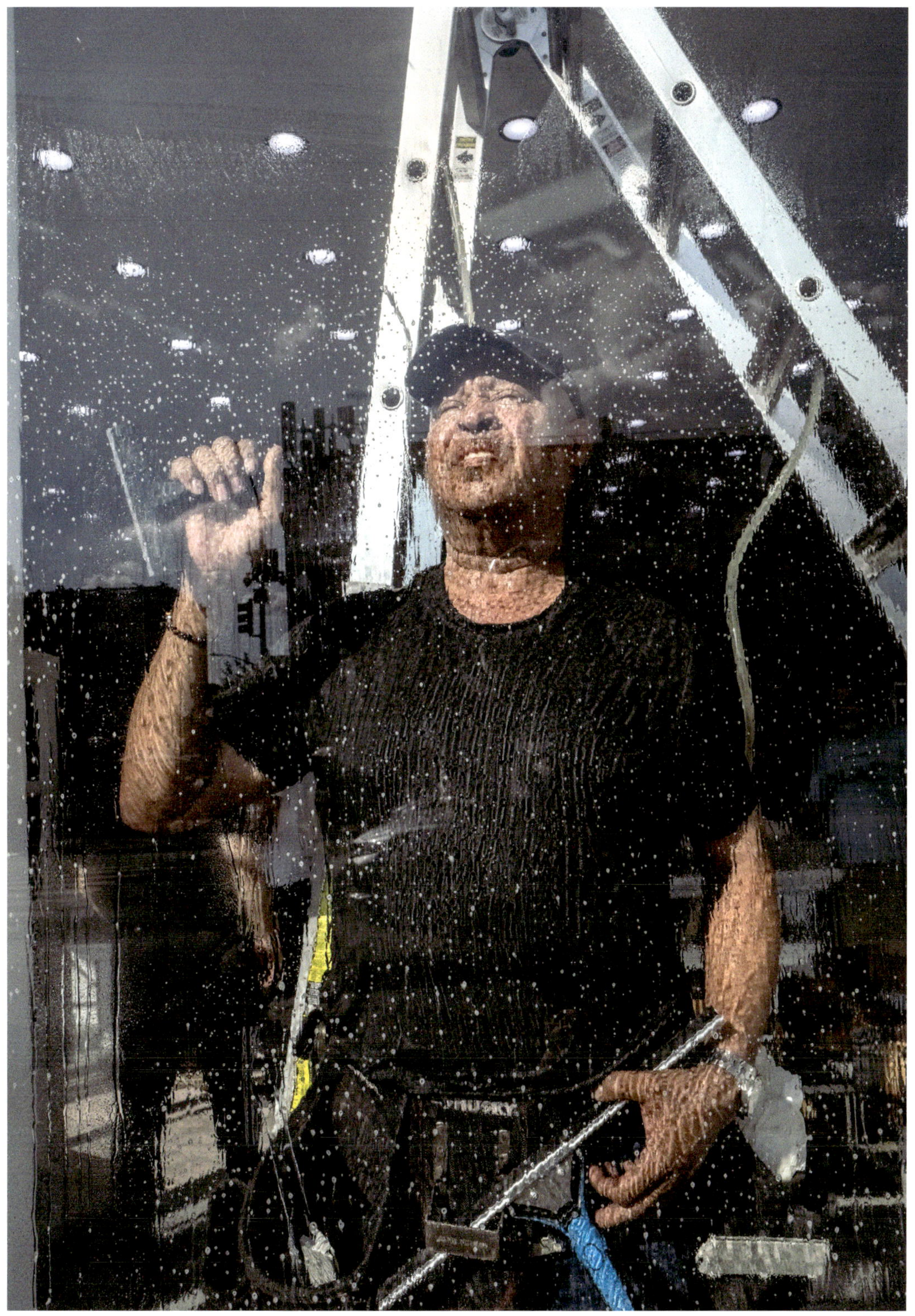

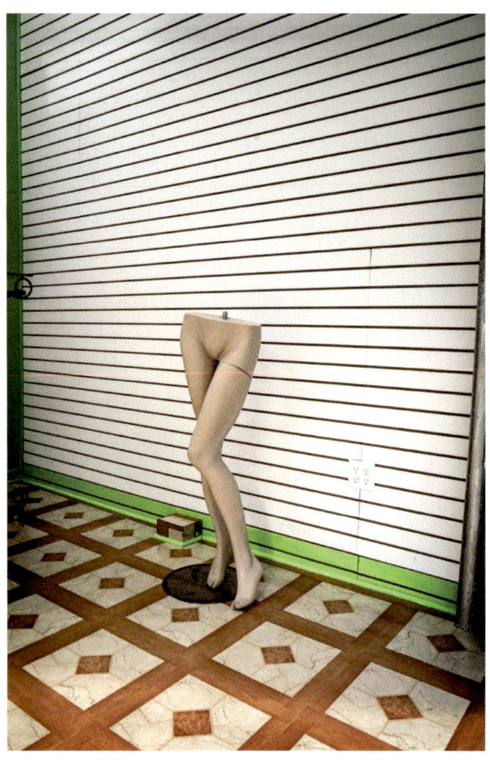

Left: The lower half of a mannequin inside a shop stall.

Below: A morning nap inside a coffee shop.

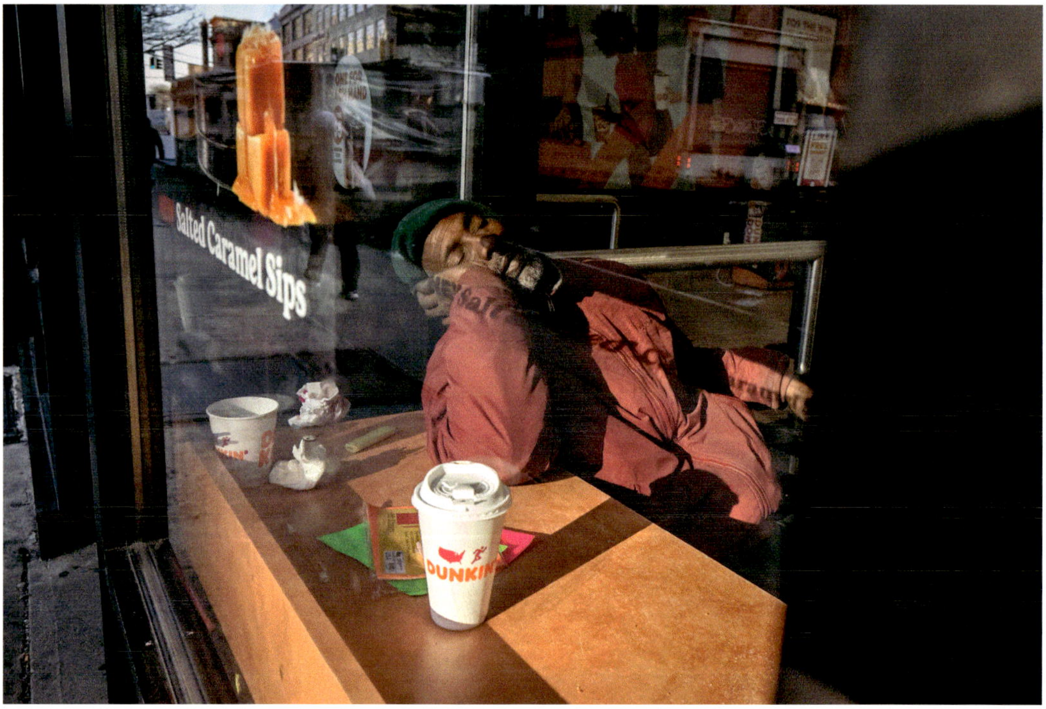

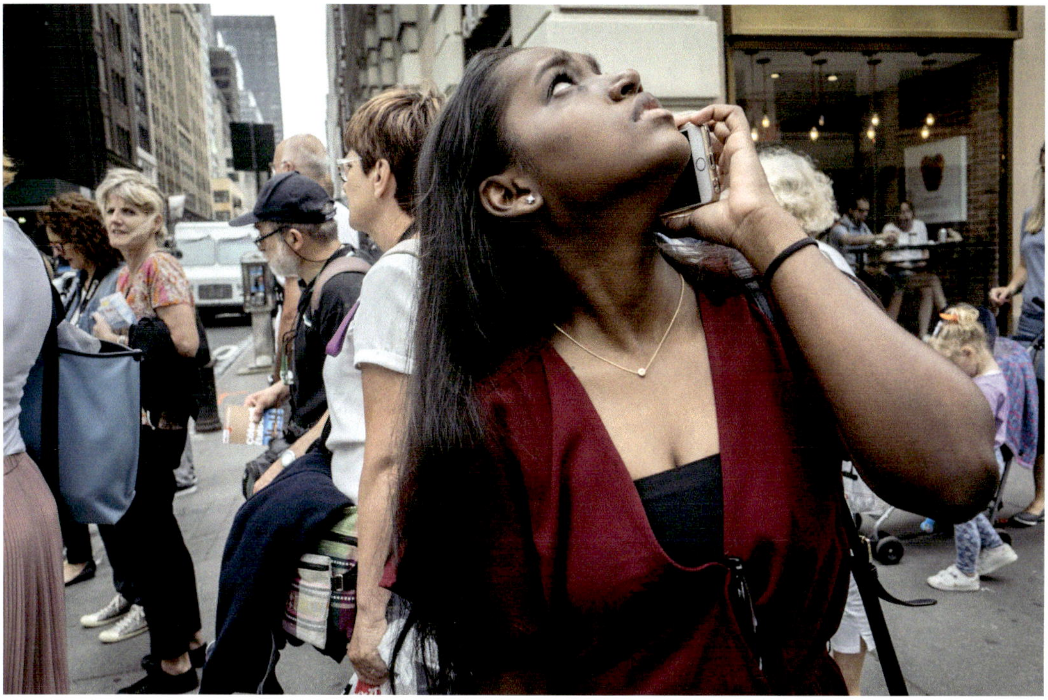

A woman looks skyward in midtown.

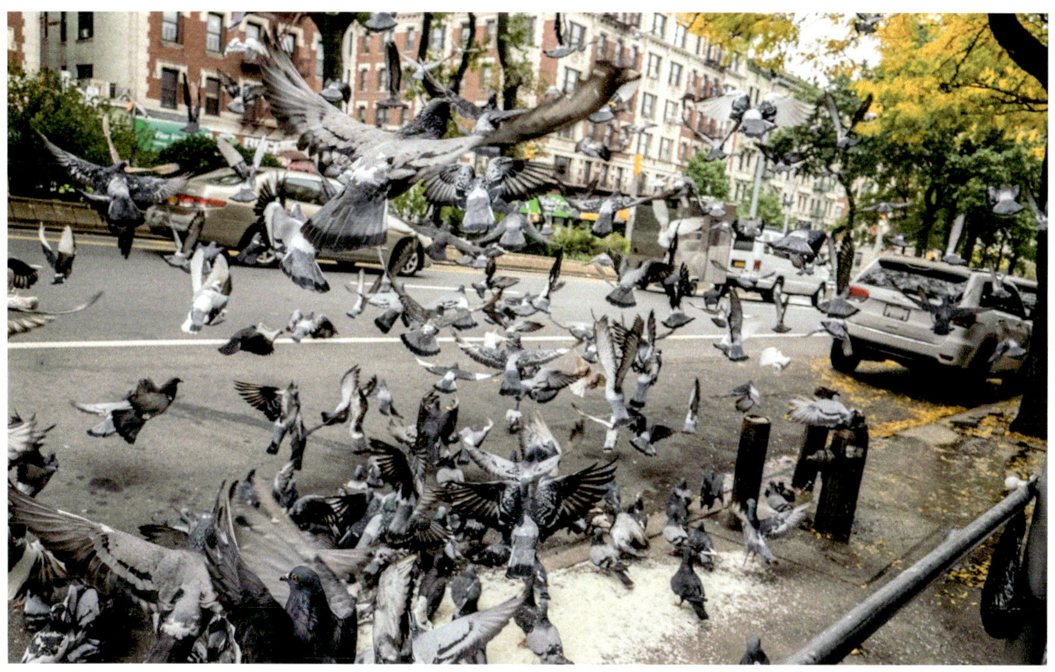

A flock of pigeons feed on rice left for them on the sidewalk.

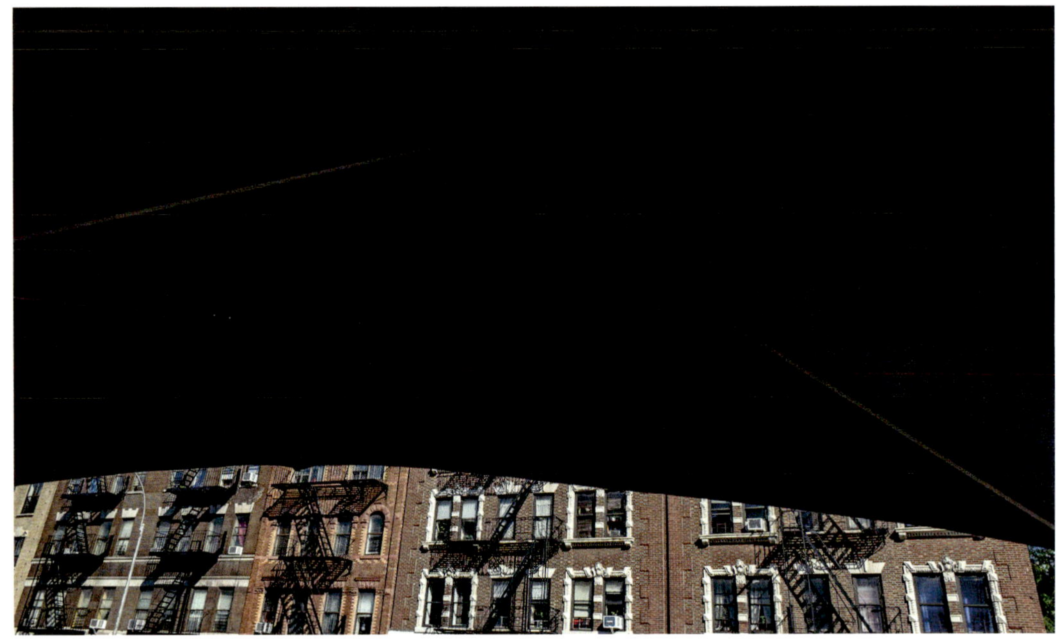

I found shelter during a quick passing drizzle on an empty street under an awning during COVID.

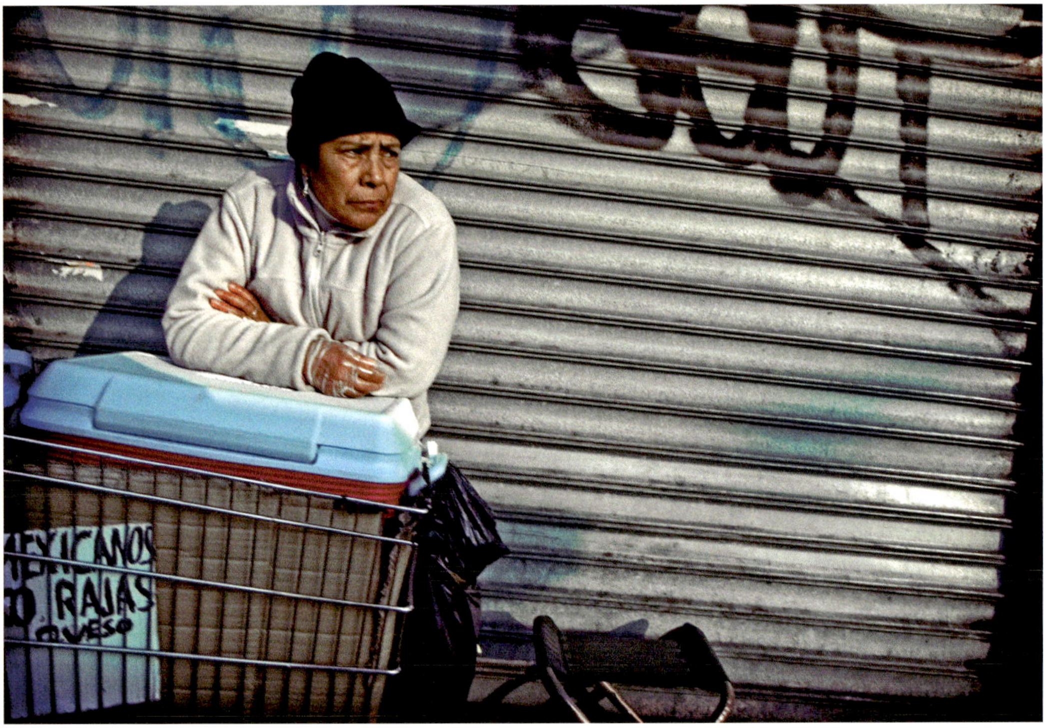

An empanada vendor.

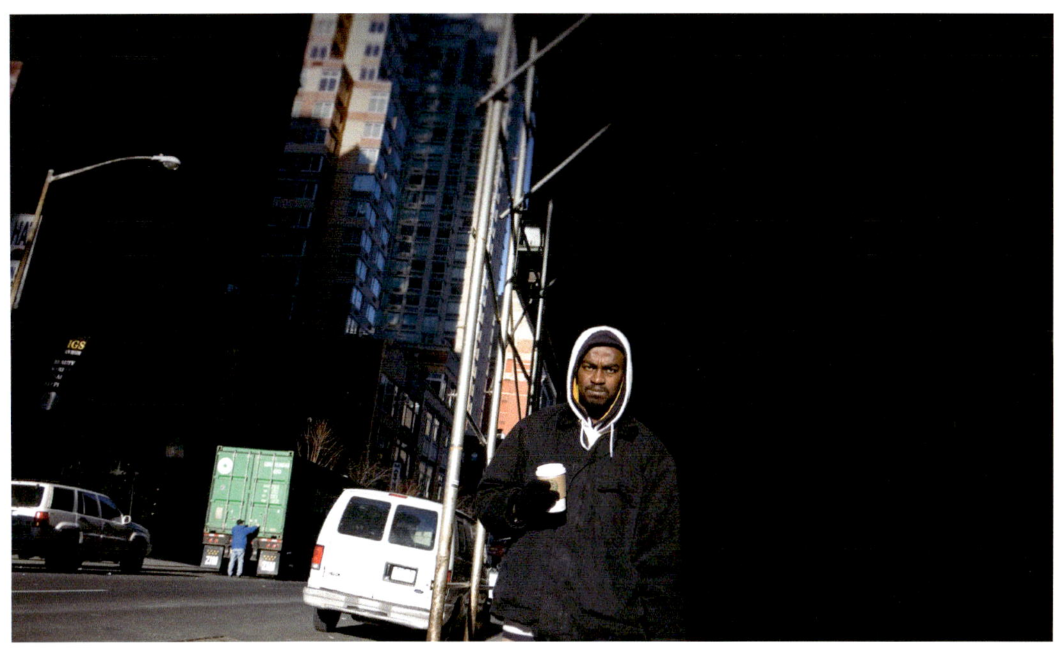

Commuter on his way to work with an early morning coffee.

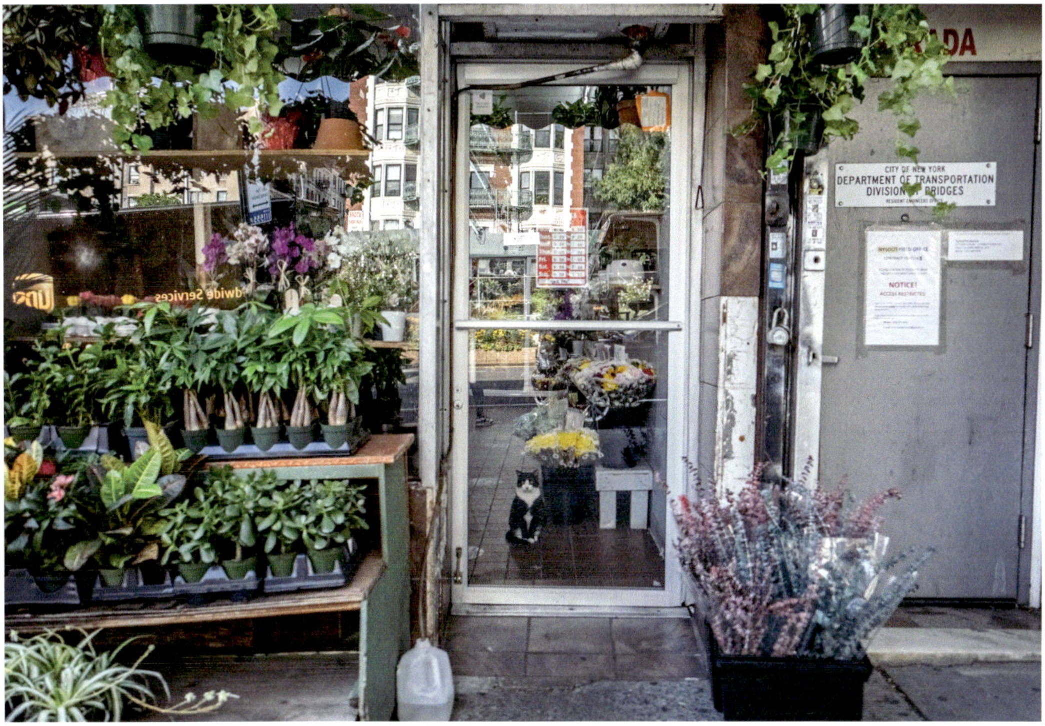

A cat in a florist's shop.

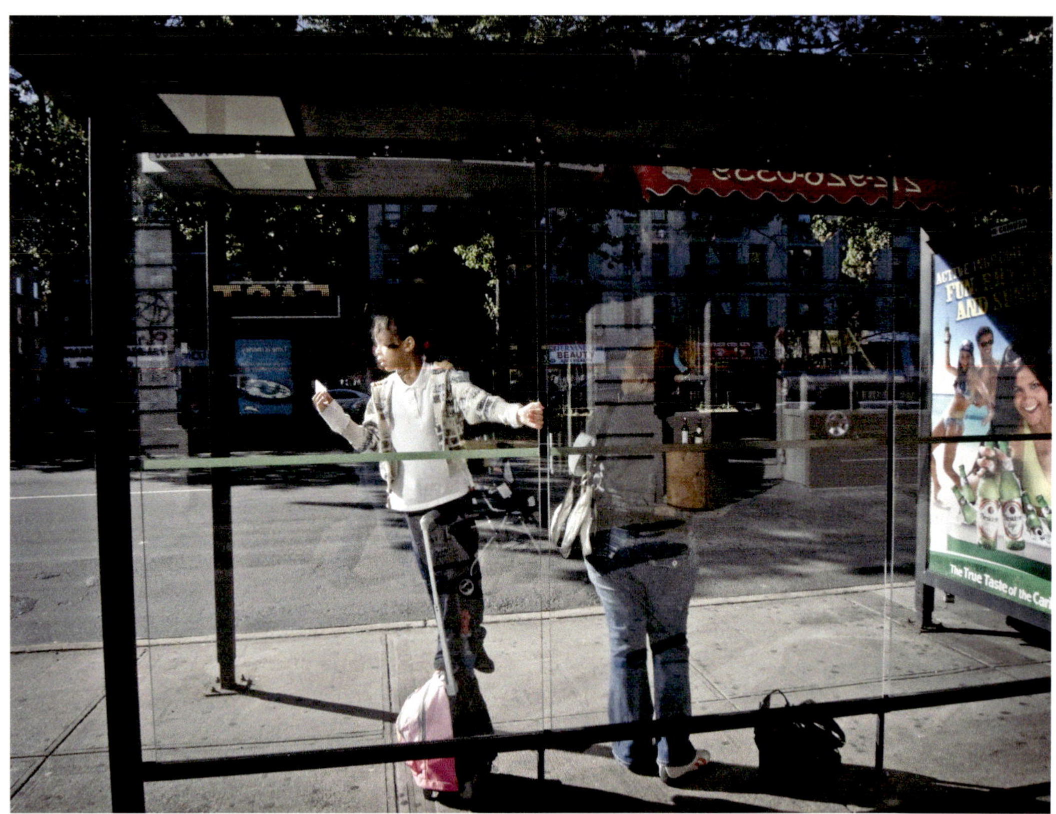

A girl waits with her mother for a bus.

Opposite page: Trinity Church, seen from Wall Street.

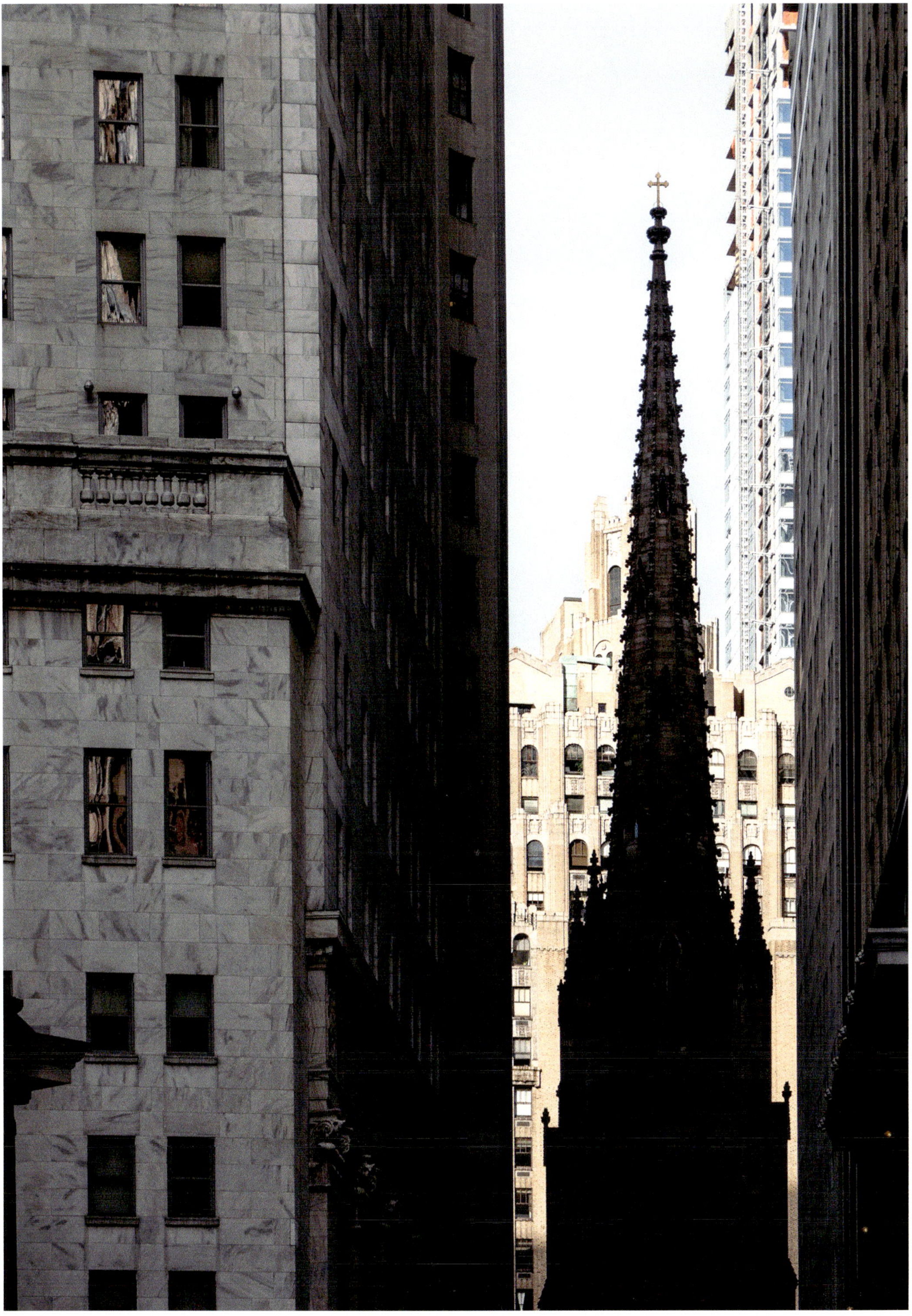

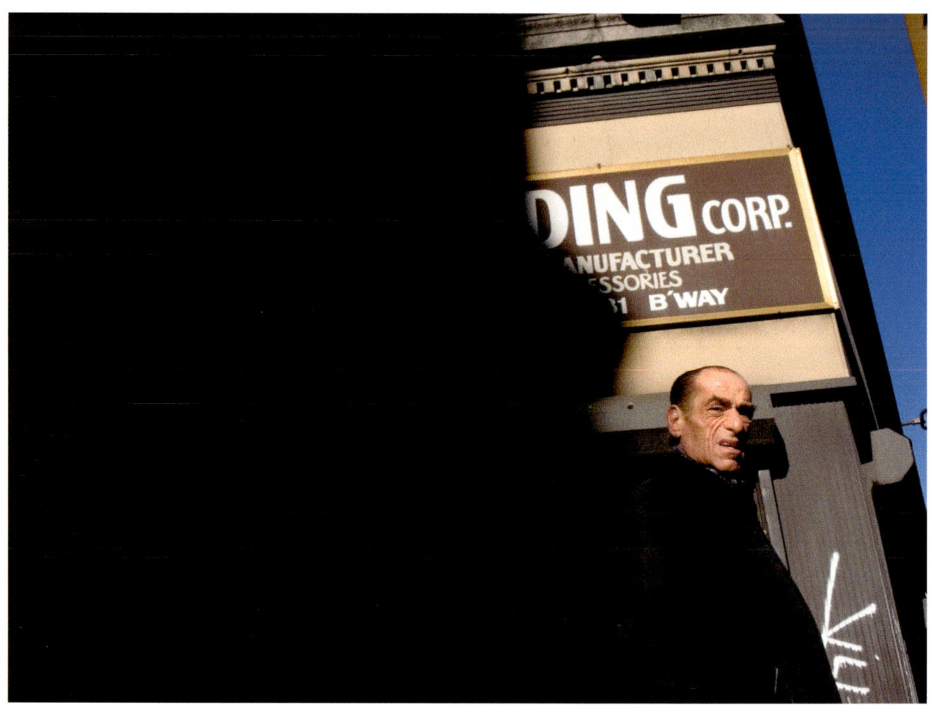

A man emerges from the morning shadows on Broadway.

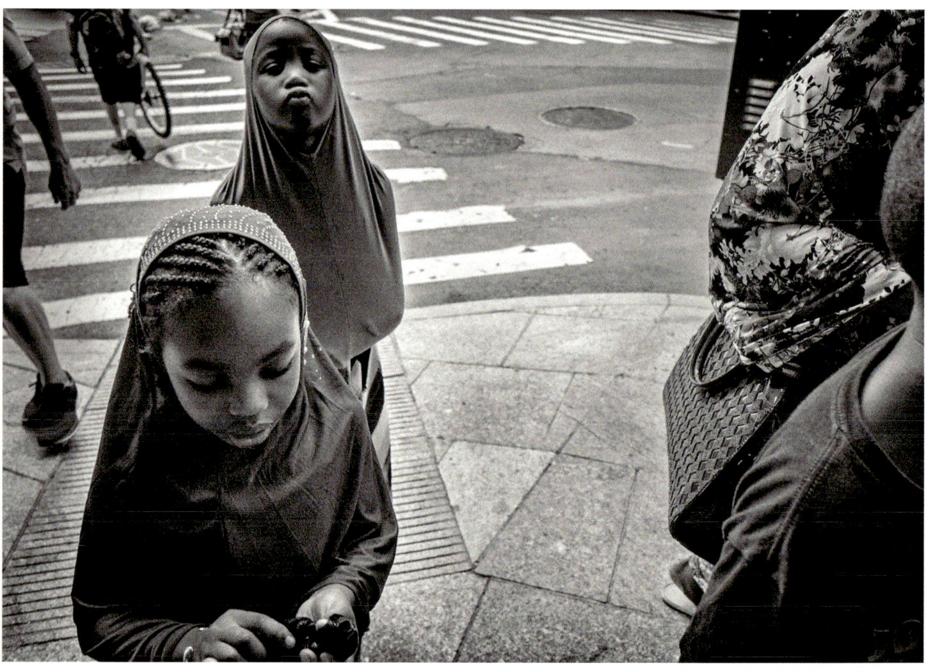

Two Muslim sisters walk up Broadway with their family.

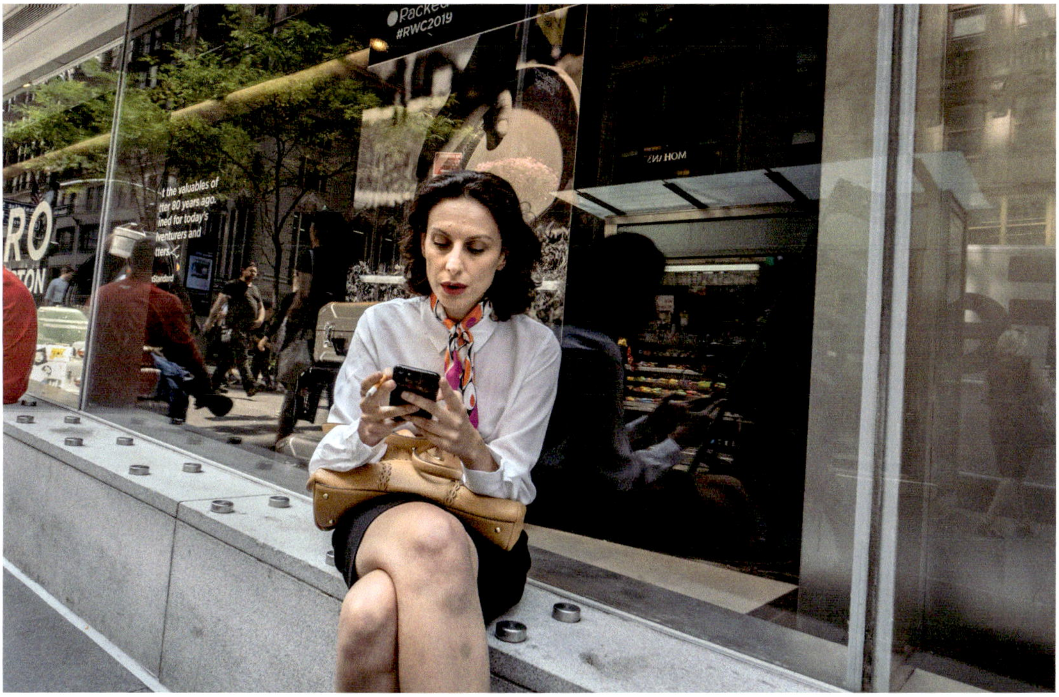

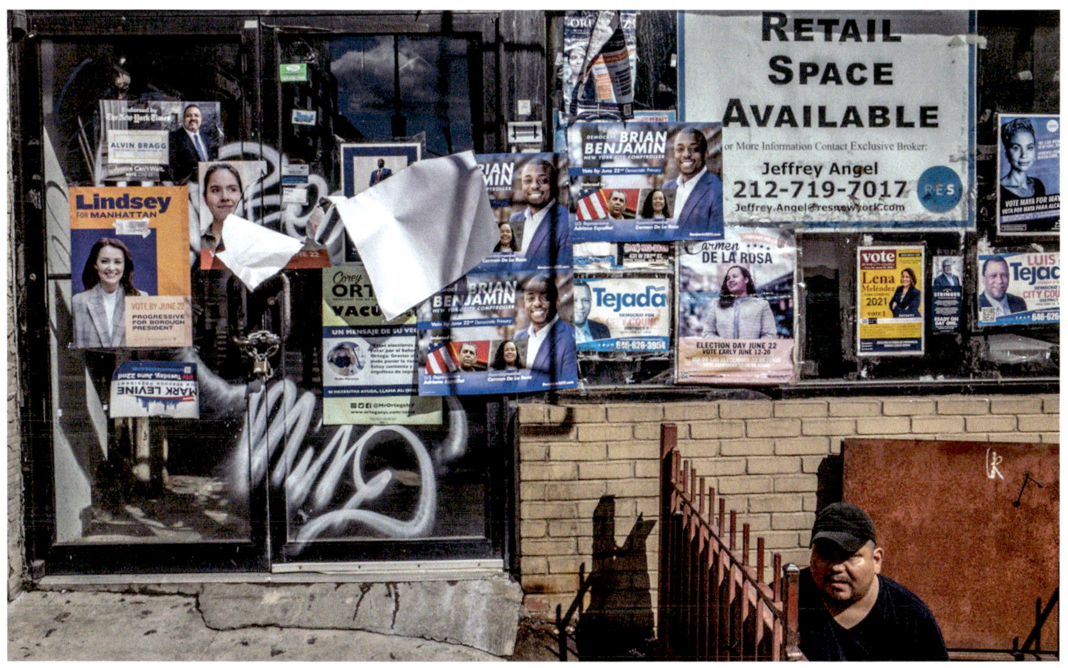

A woman checks her cell phone on her lunchtime.

A man emerges from the basement of a store for rent.

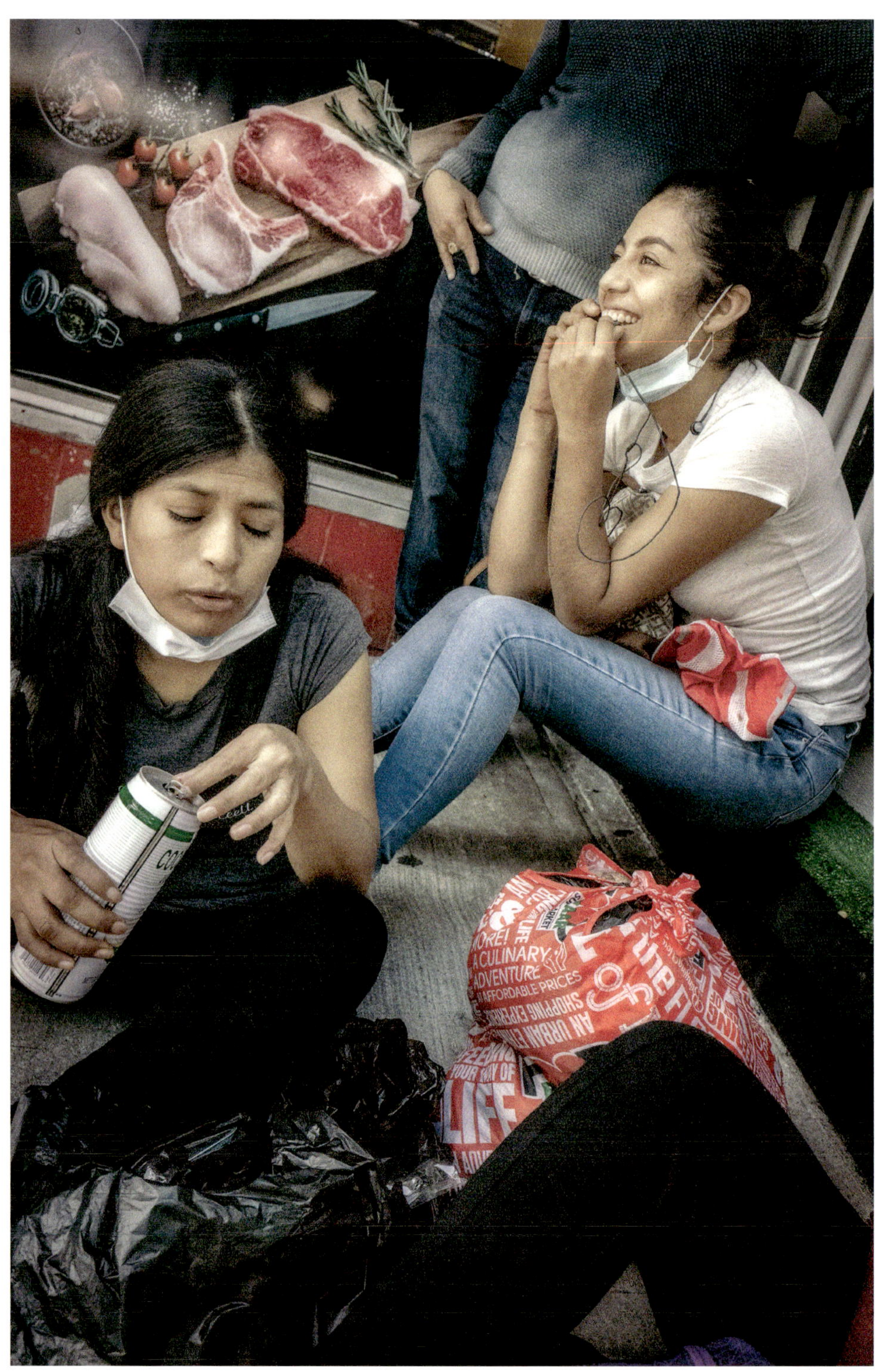

A group of girls share a laugh and drinks during COVID.

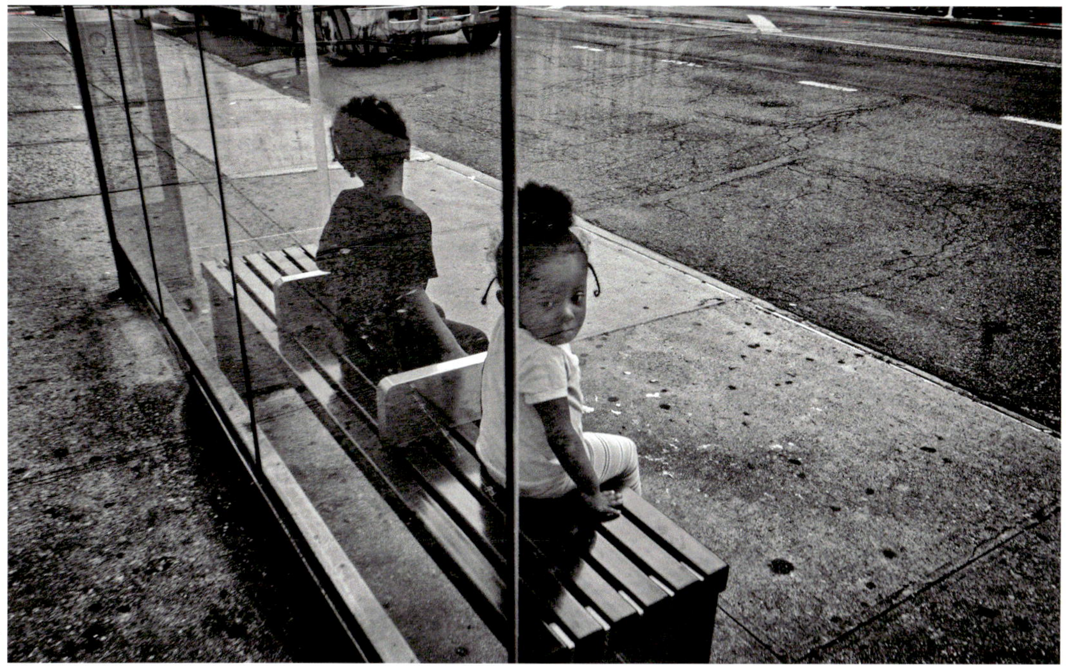

Two children wait at a bus stop, while one looks at her mother.

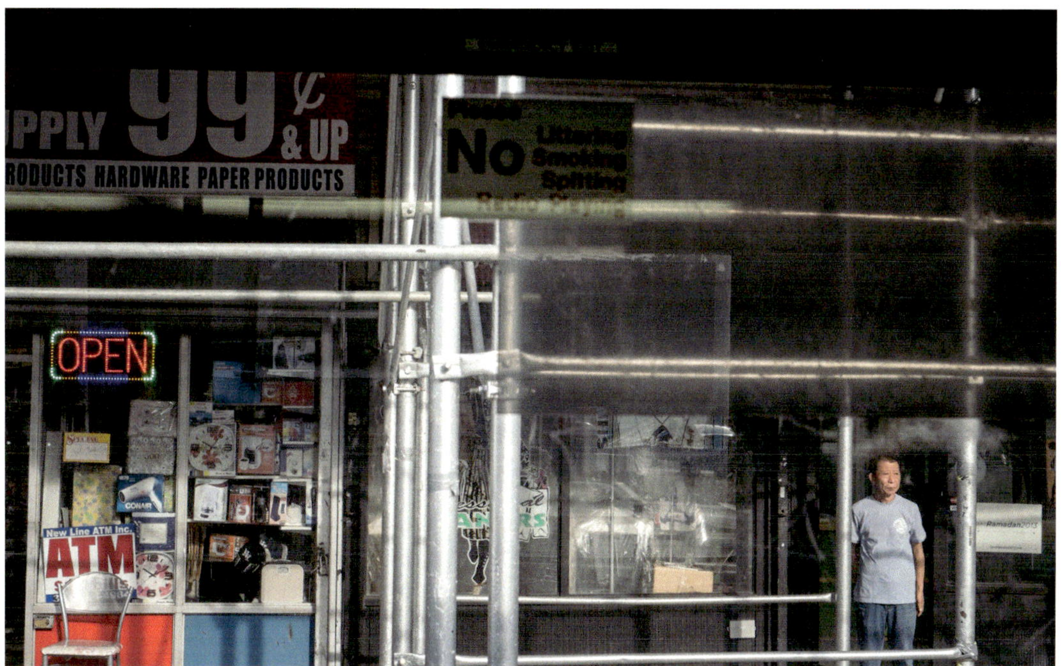

On the first day of Ramadan, I was riding a bus when the geometric patterns of the construction shed pillars caught my eye, framing a man gazing through them.

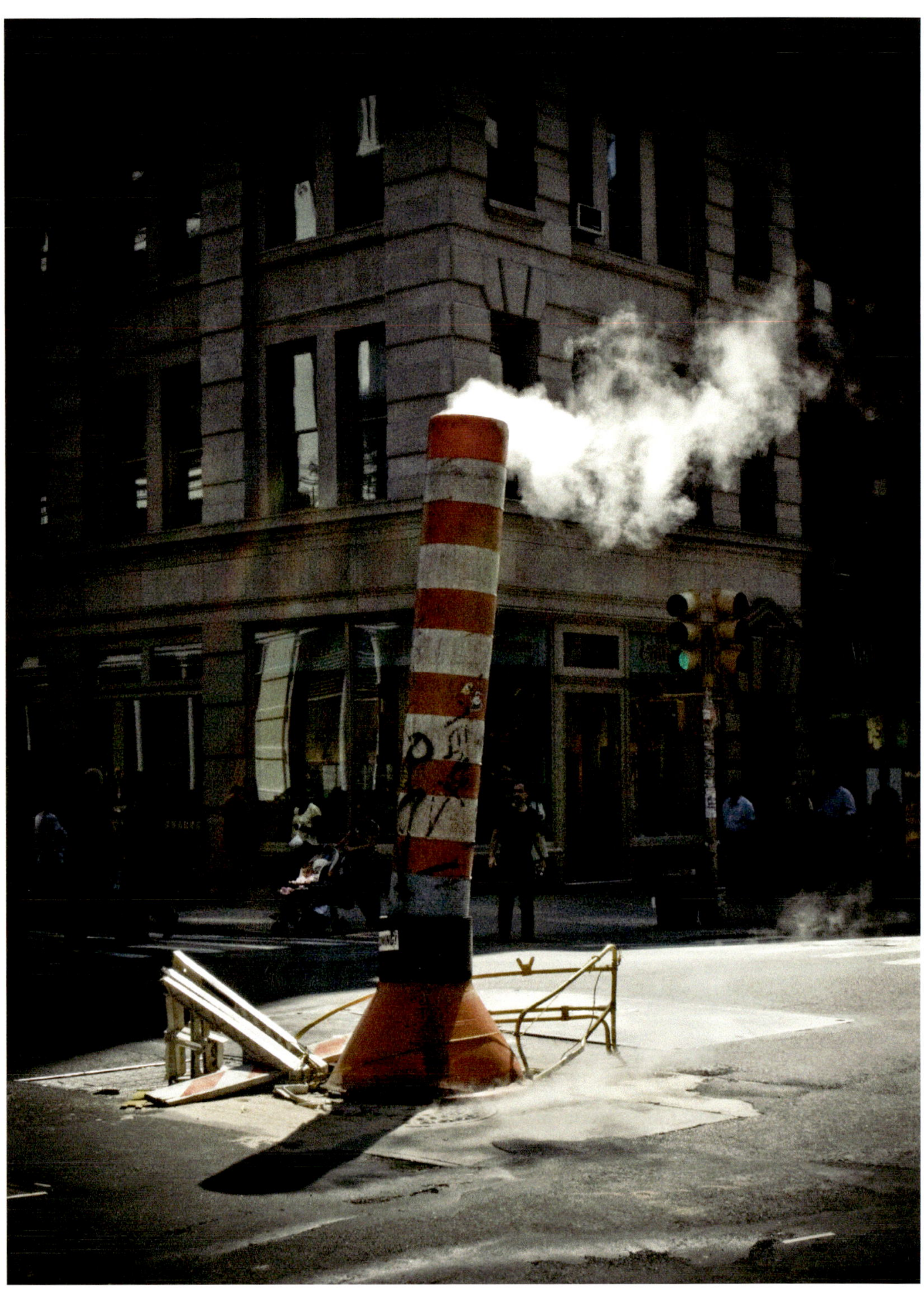

A stream vent in the middle of Broadway.

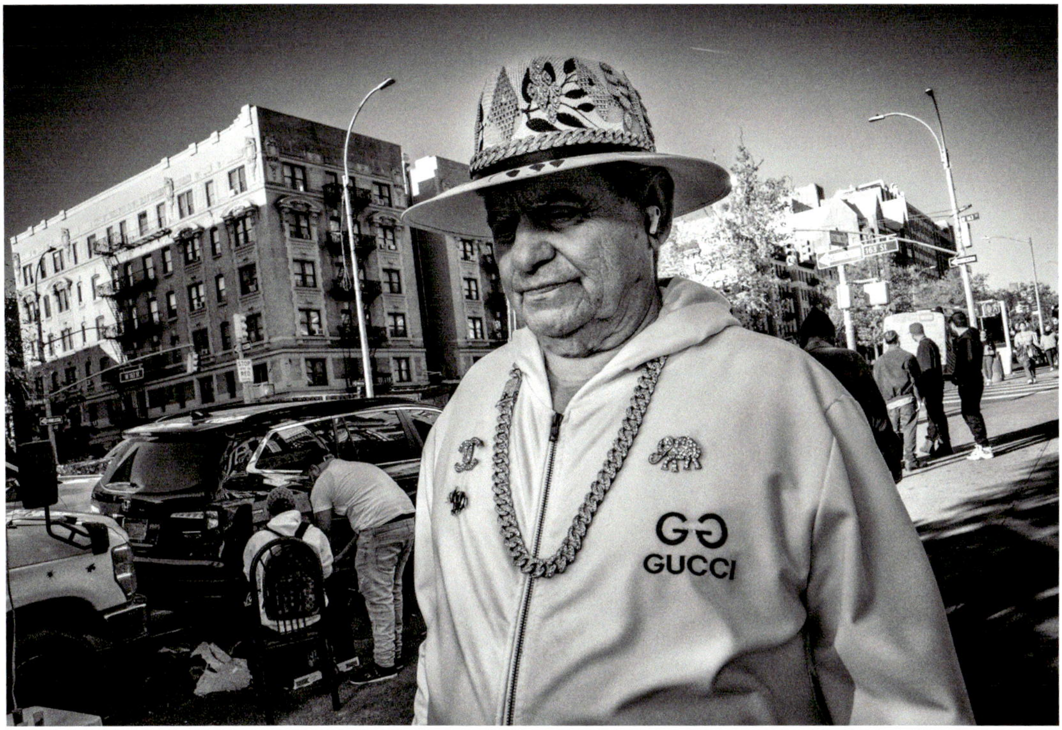

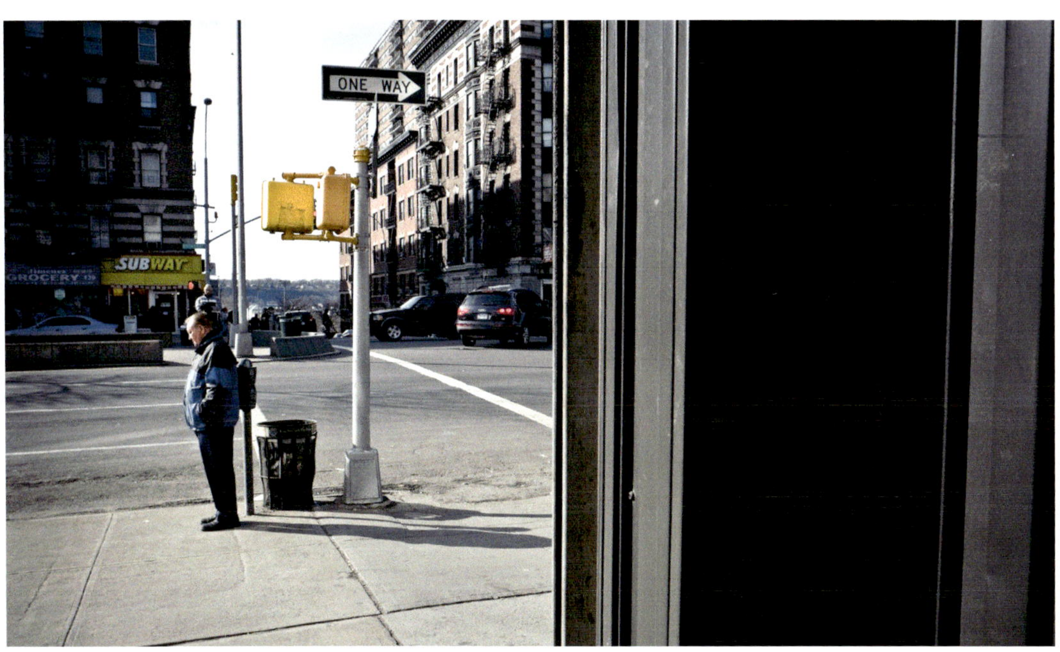

A man outfitted in Gucci.

A pensive moment while waiting for the crosswalk light to change.

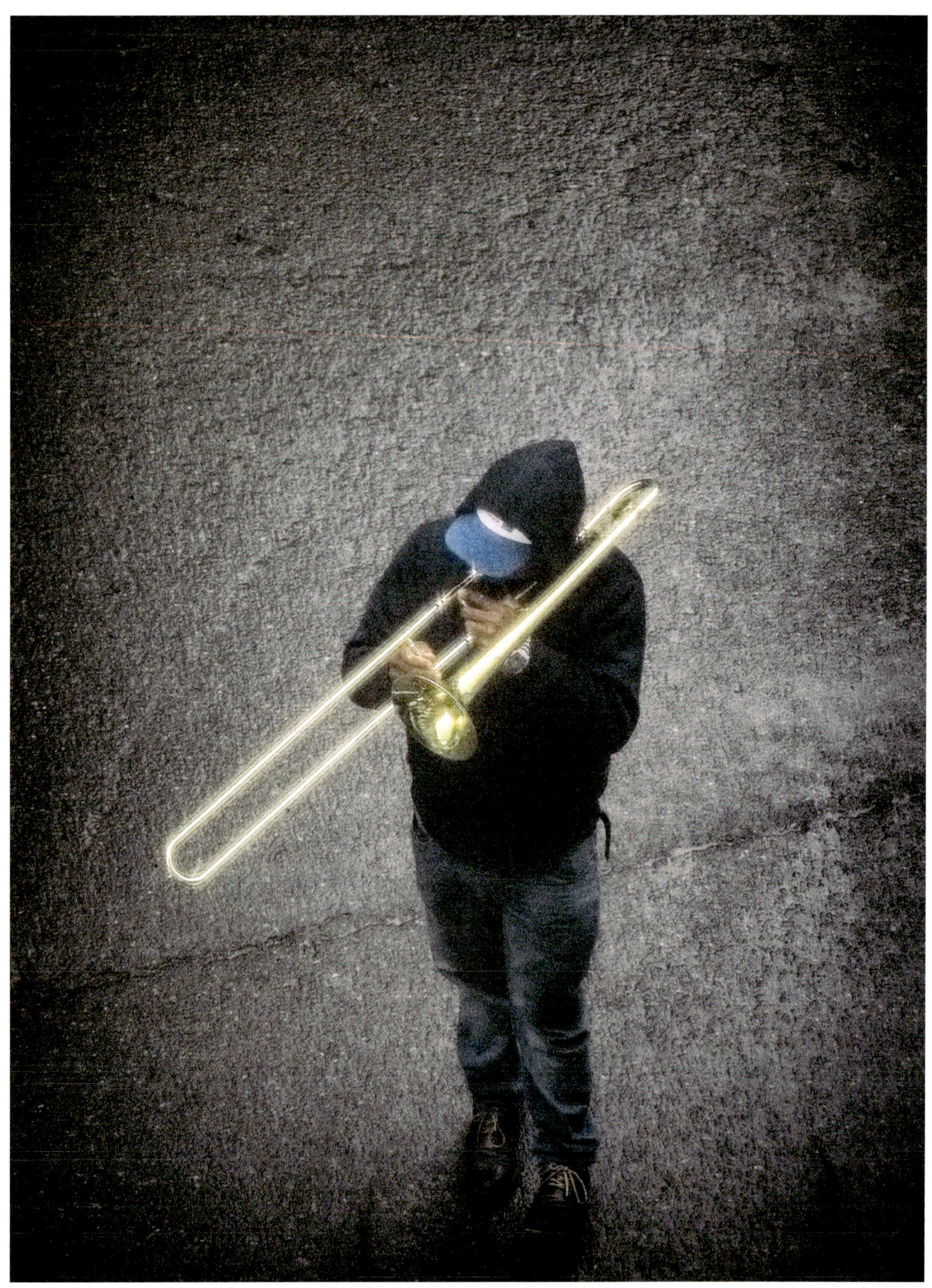

Playing trombone during a Dominican presidential parade.

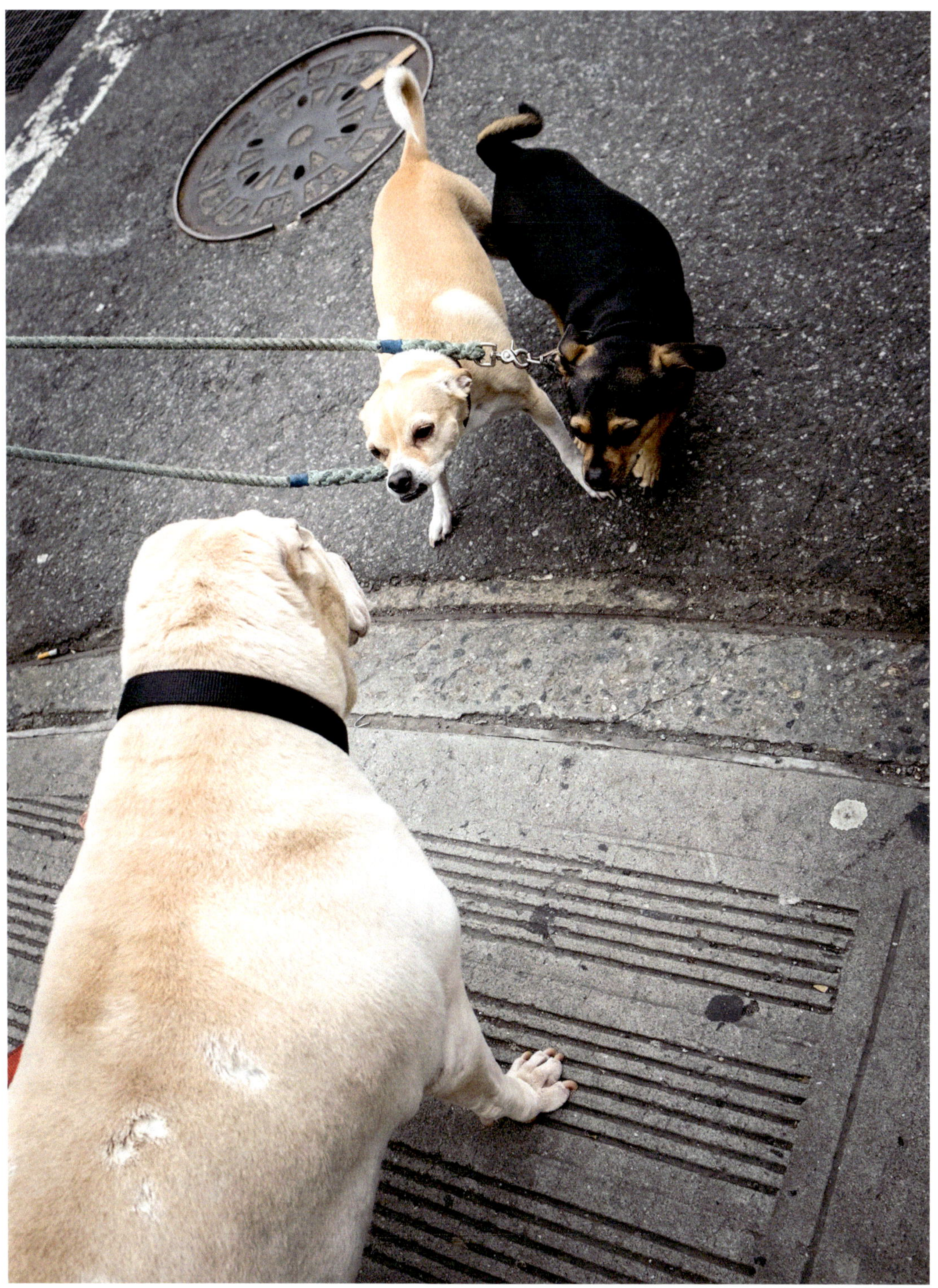

Dogs meet during their walk.

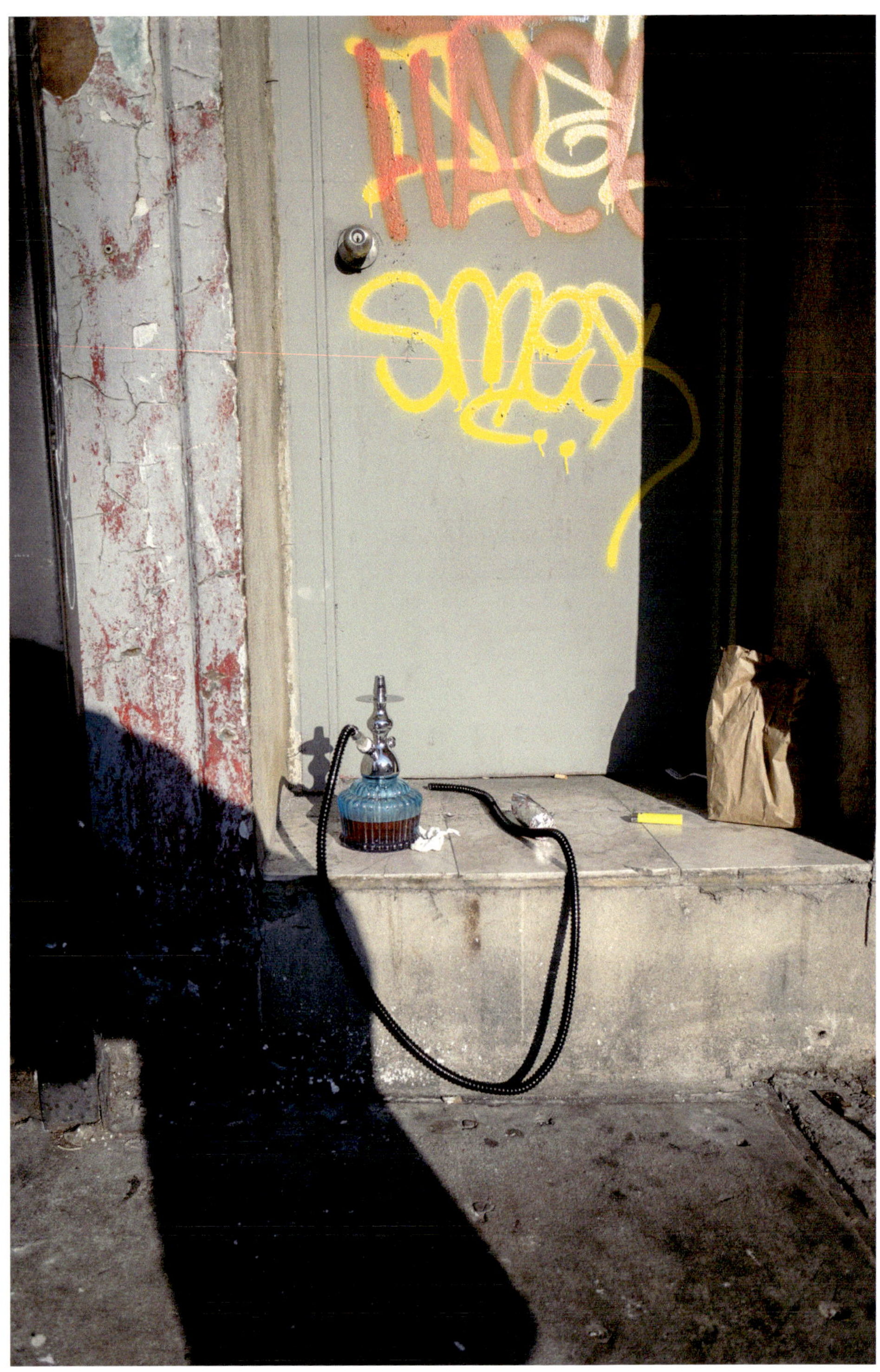

A water pipe left in a doorway.

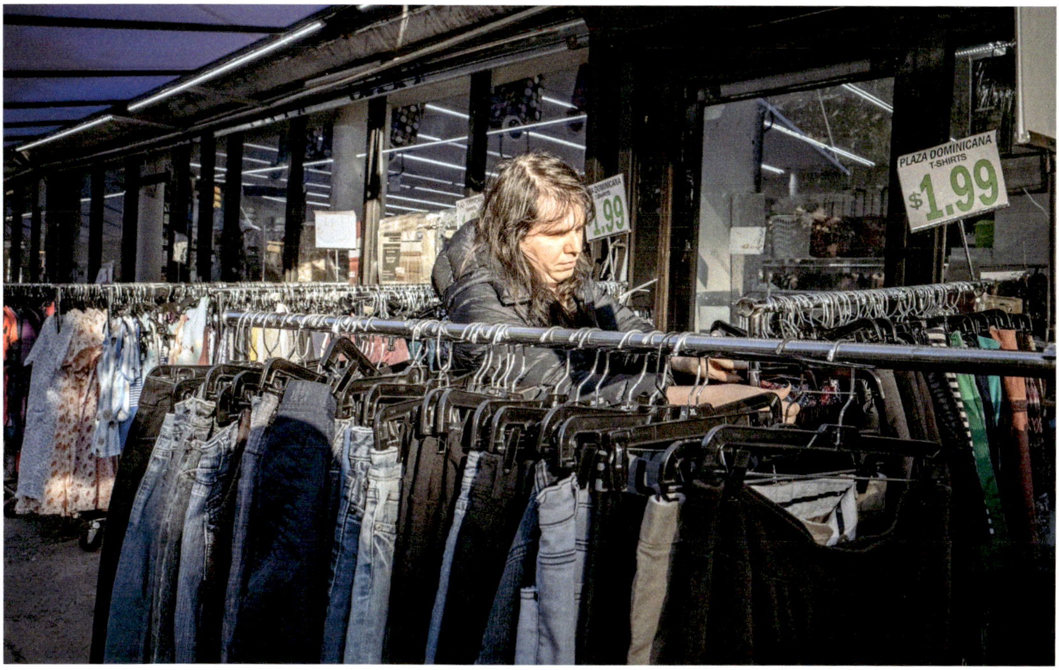

A woman searches through a rack of clothing of an outlet store.

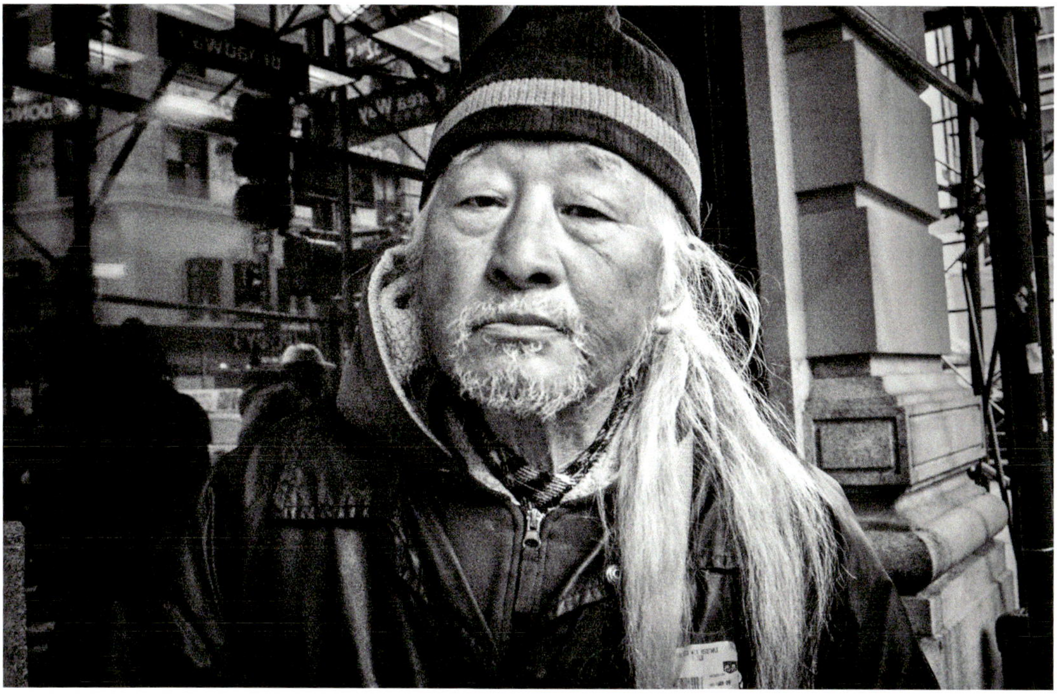

Portrait of a homeless man near Korea Town.

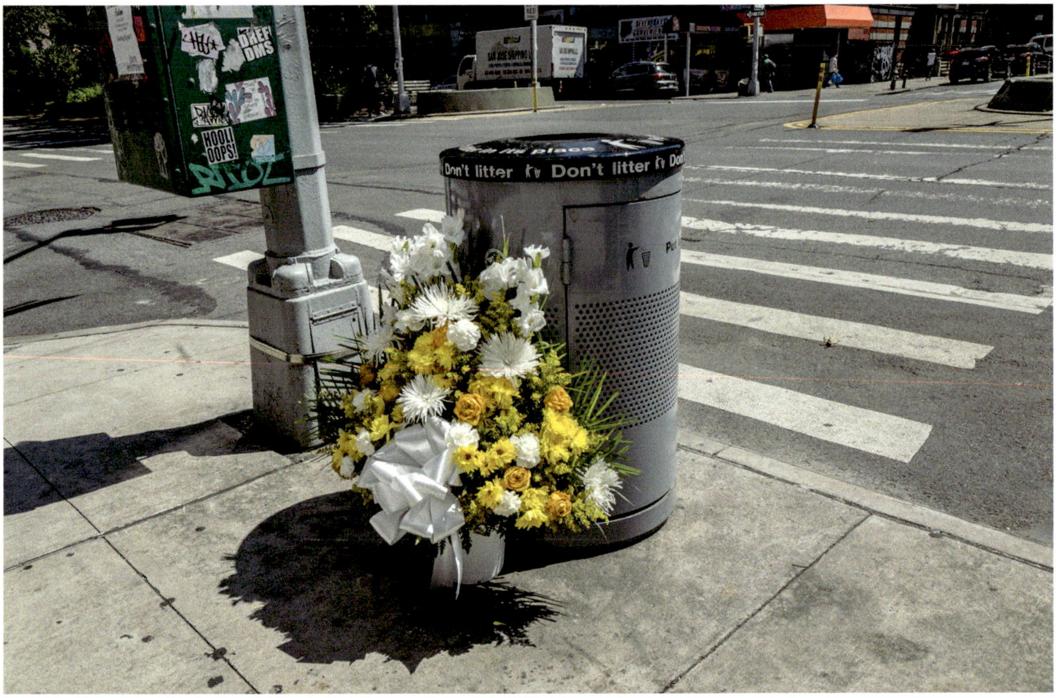

Abandoned bouquet of flowers.

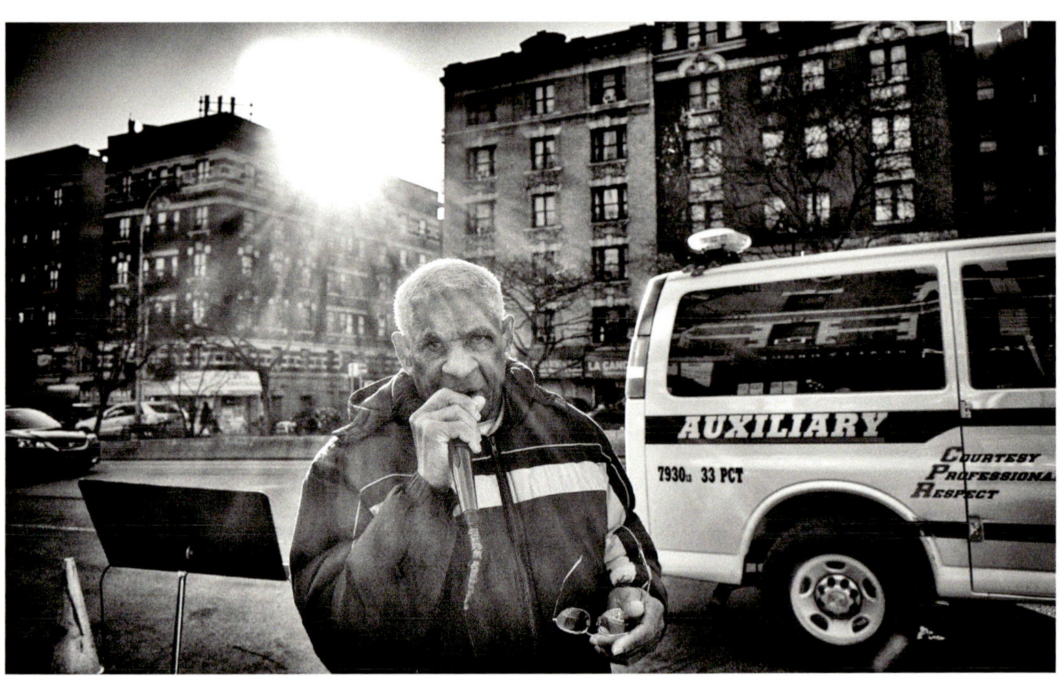

A sidewalk evangelist.

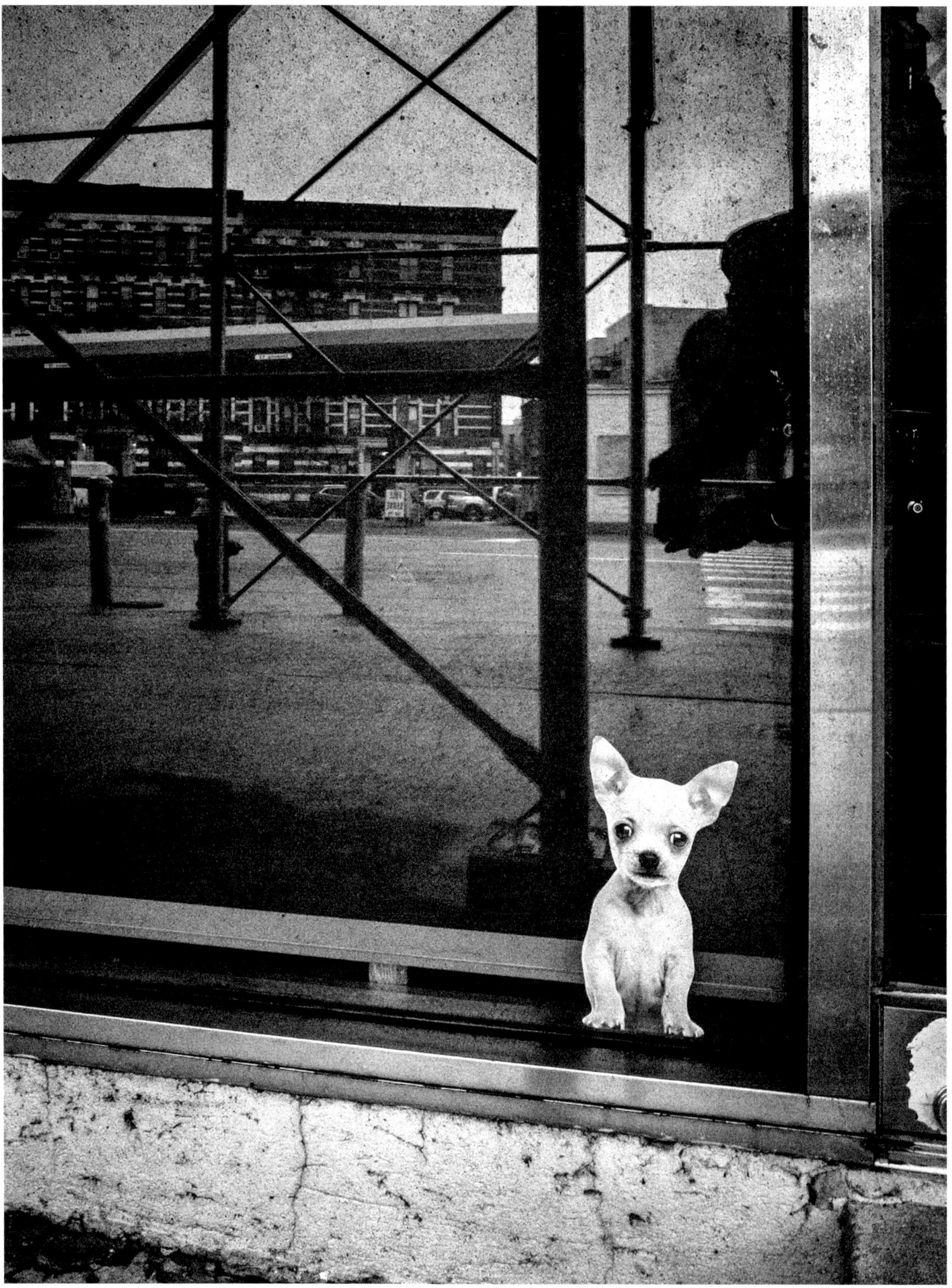

Walking down Broadway, I saw what I thought was a little dog in a window of an empty store. As I got closer, I realized it was just a cutout picture.

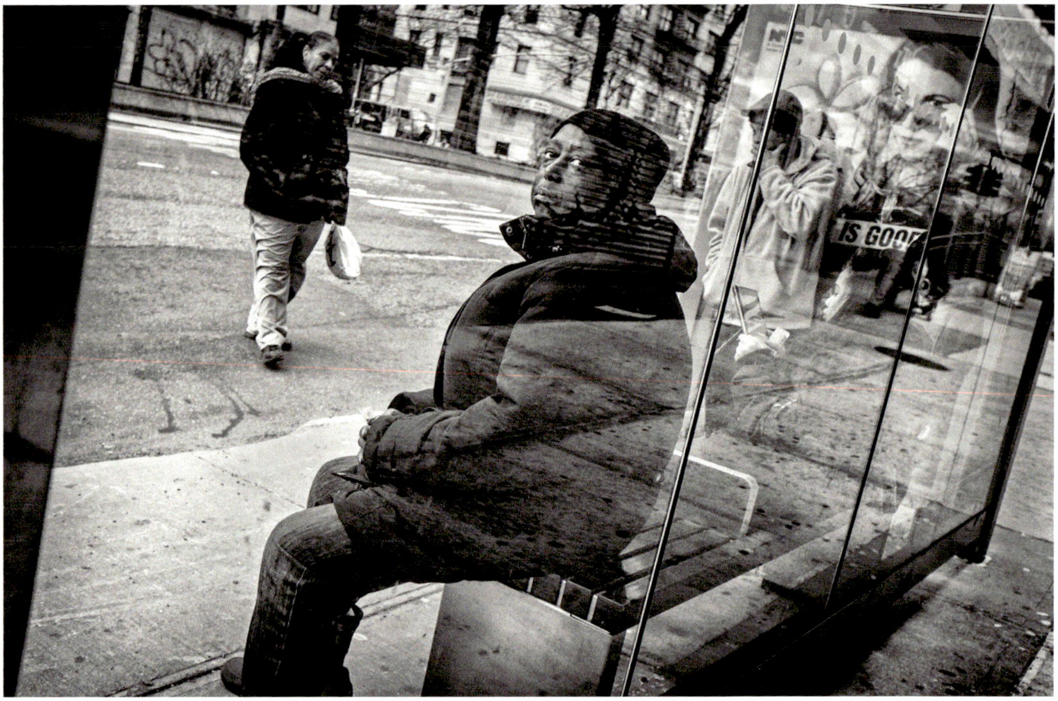

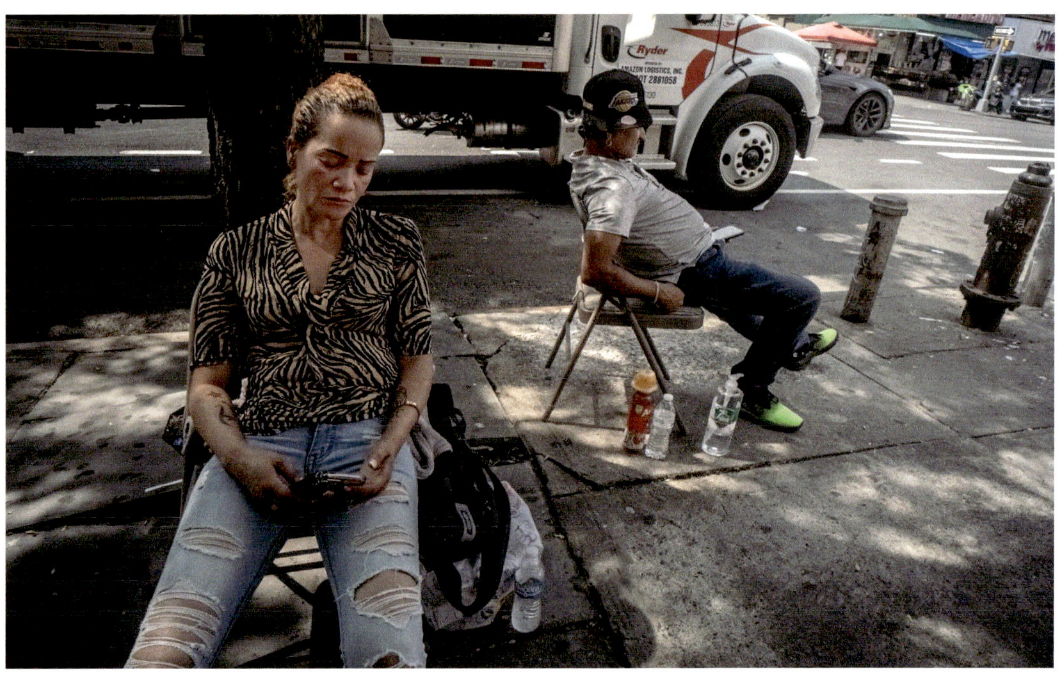

Bus stop reflections. (Yes, I am fond of the image opportunities at bus stop kiosks!)

A couple hangs out on a steamy afternoon.

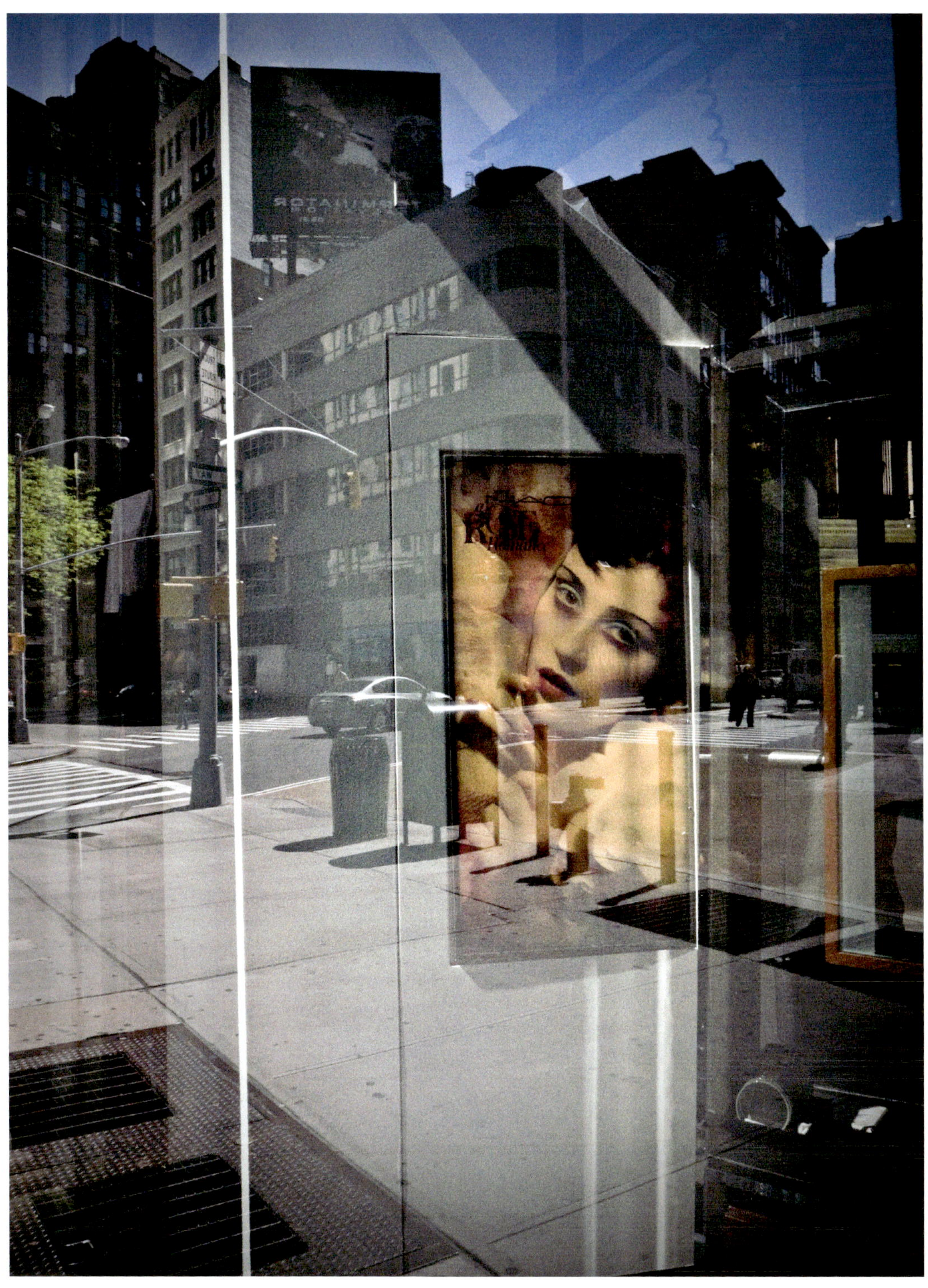

A face and window reflections.

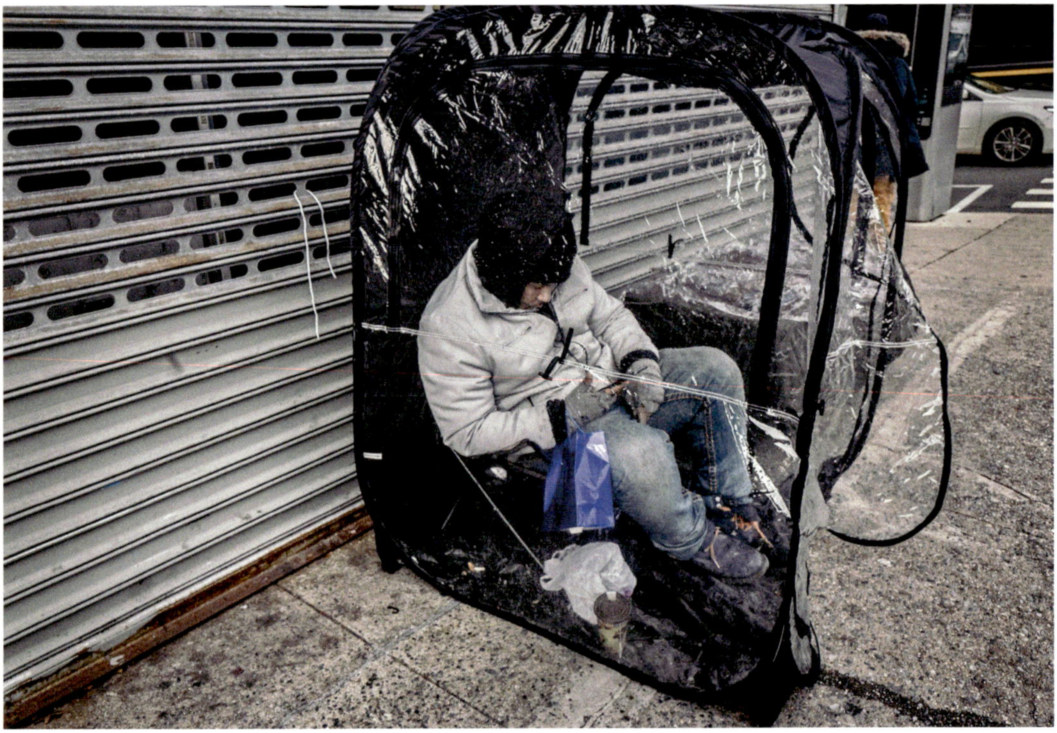

A vendor shielded from the wind in a bubble on a cold day.

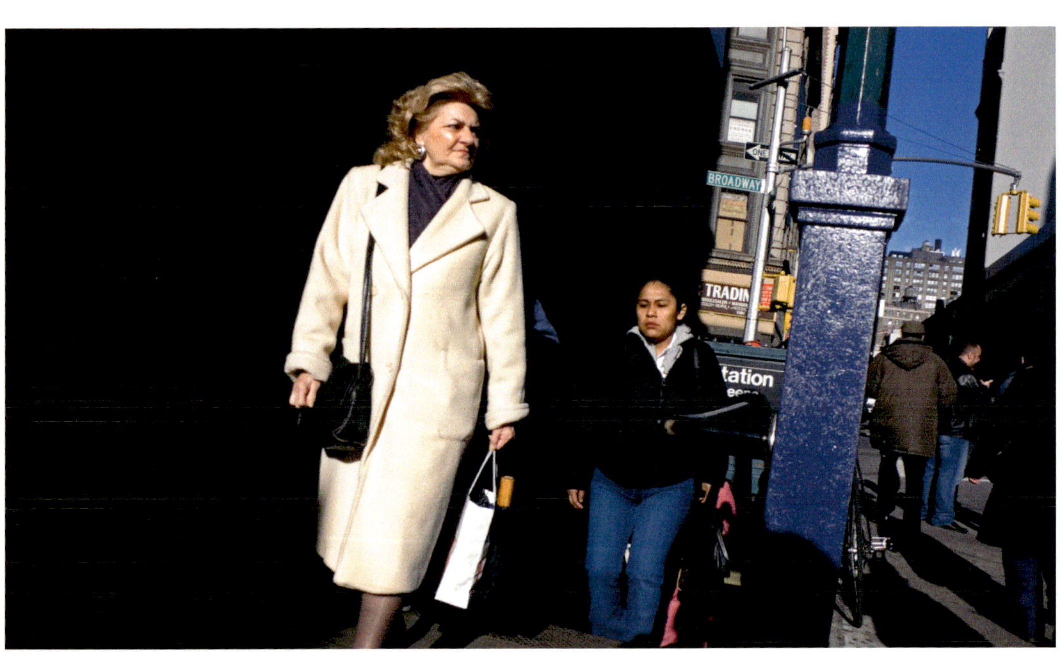

Commuters exit from the subway.

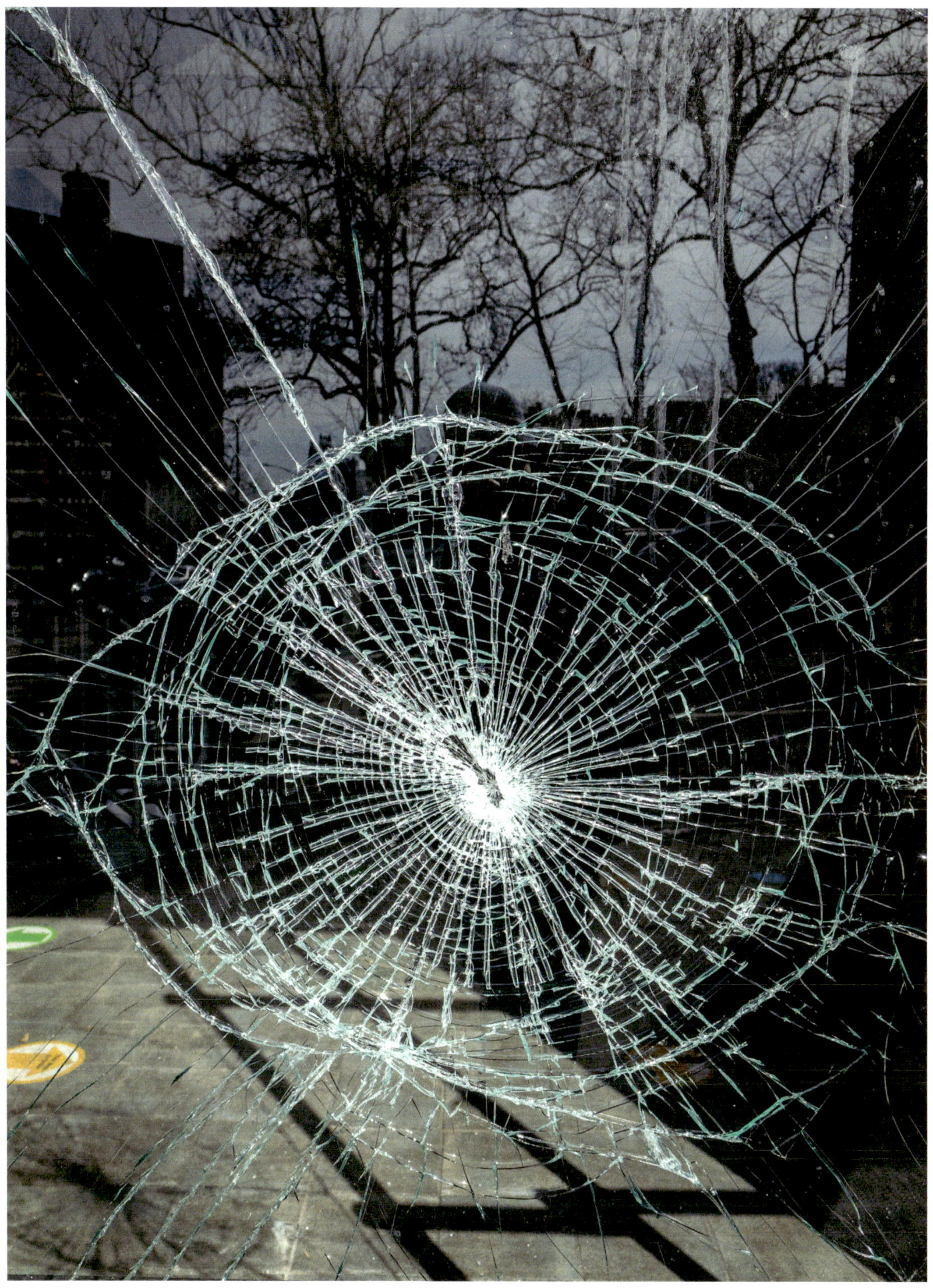

Smashed bank window.

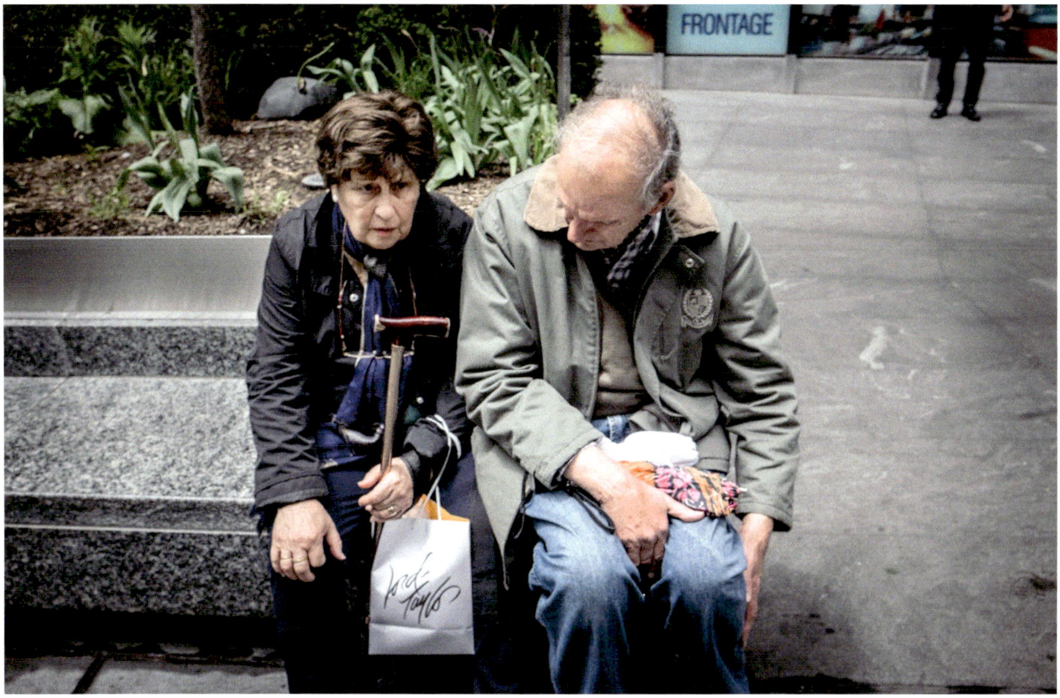

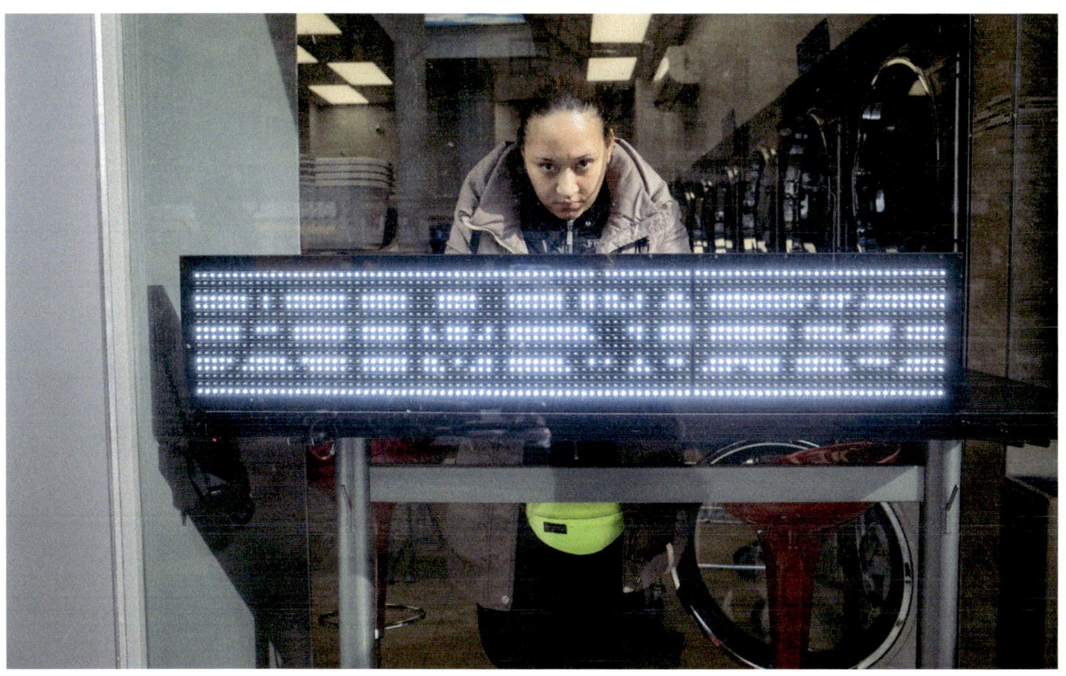

A senior couple takes a break in a small office park.

Woman in laundromat.

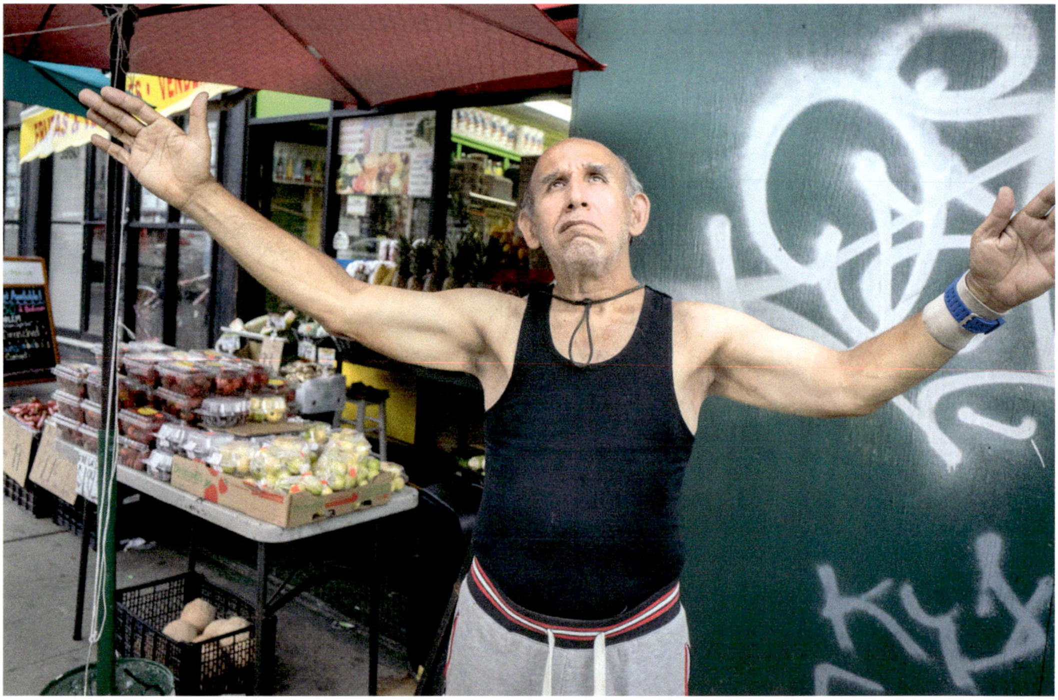

A man gives prayer.

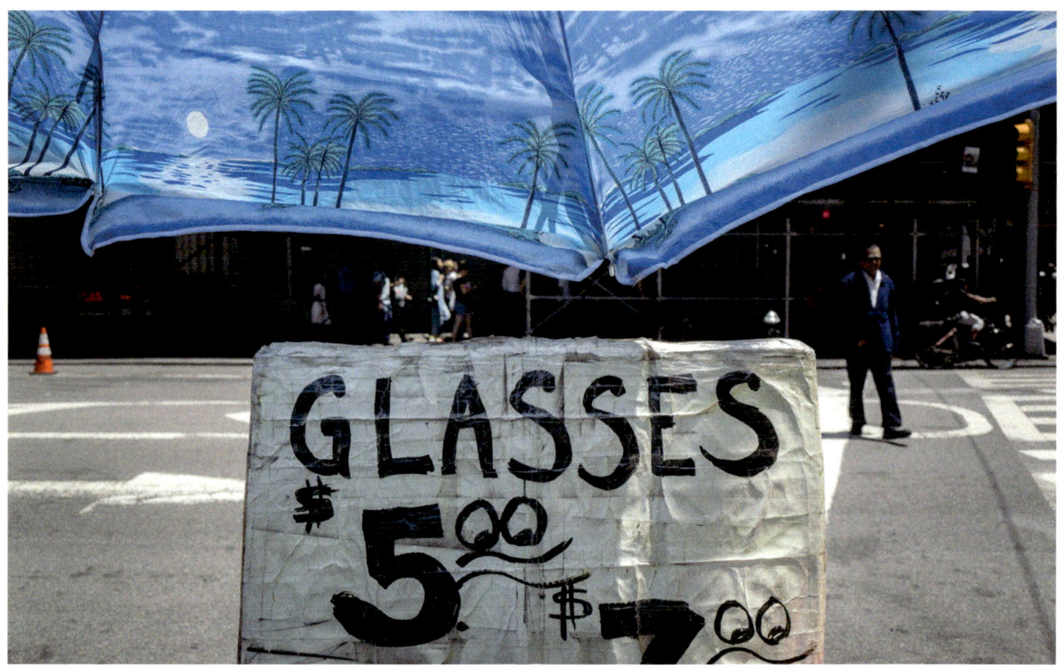

A sunglass vendor's stall.

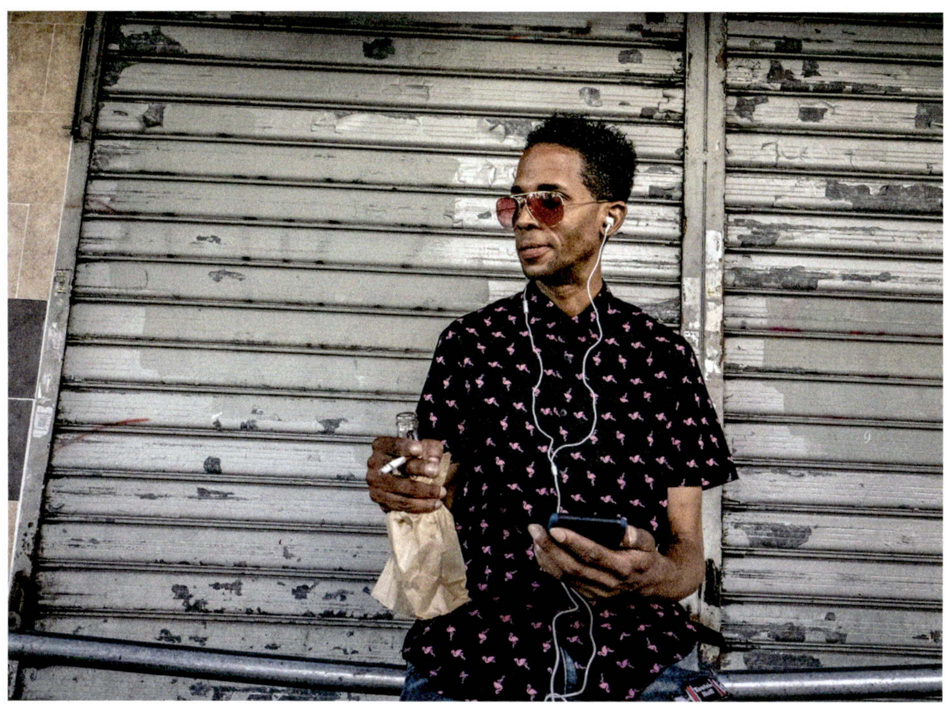

Pink flamingos.

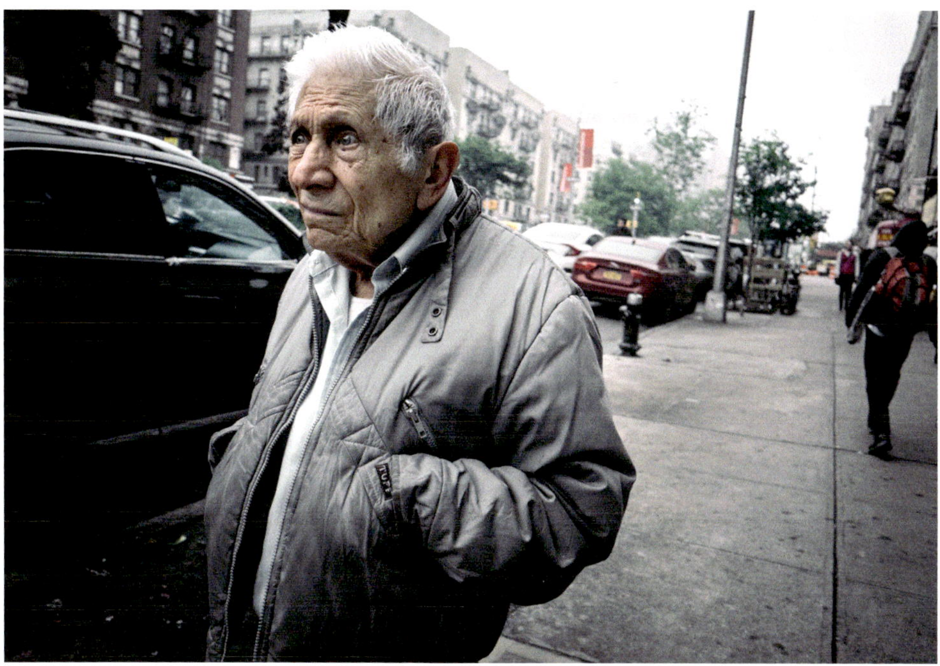

Senior man strolling down Broadway.

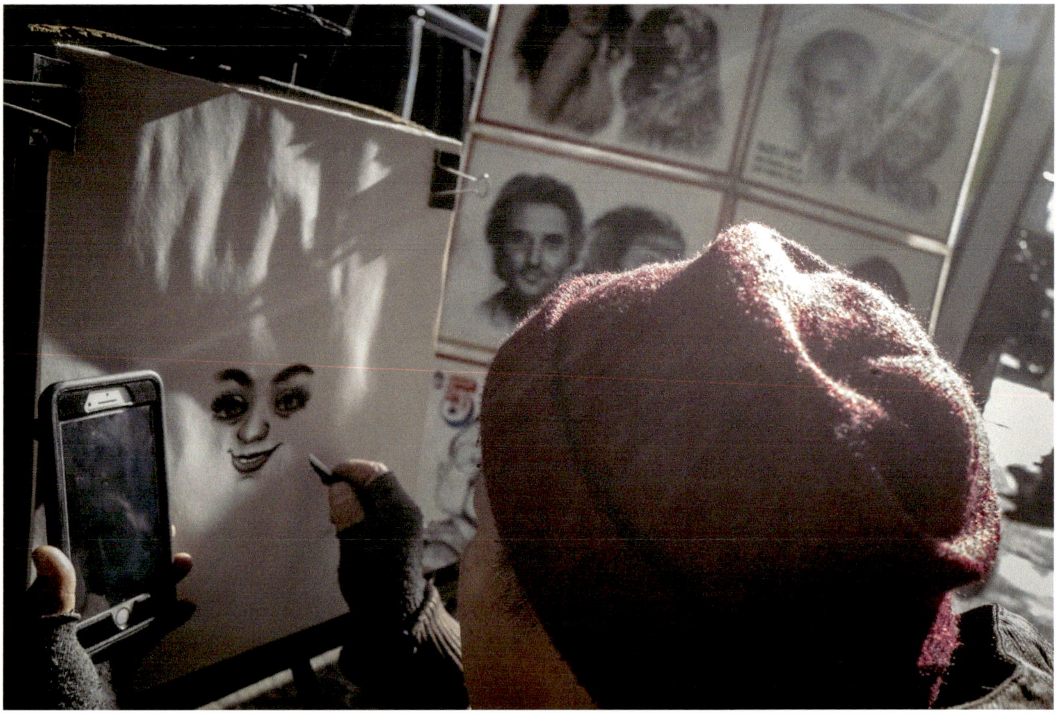

A street artist draws a portrait from a cell phone.

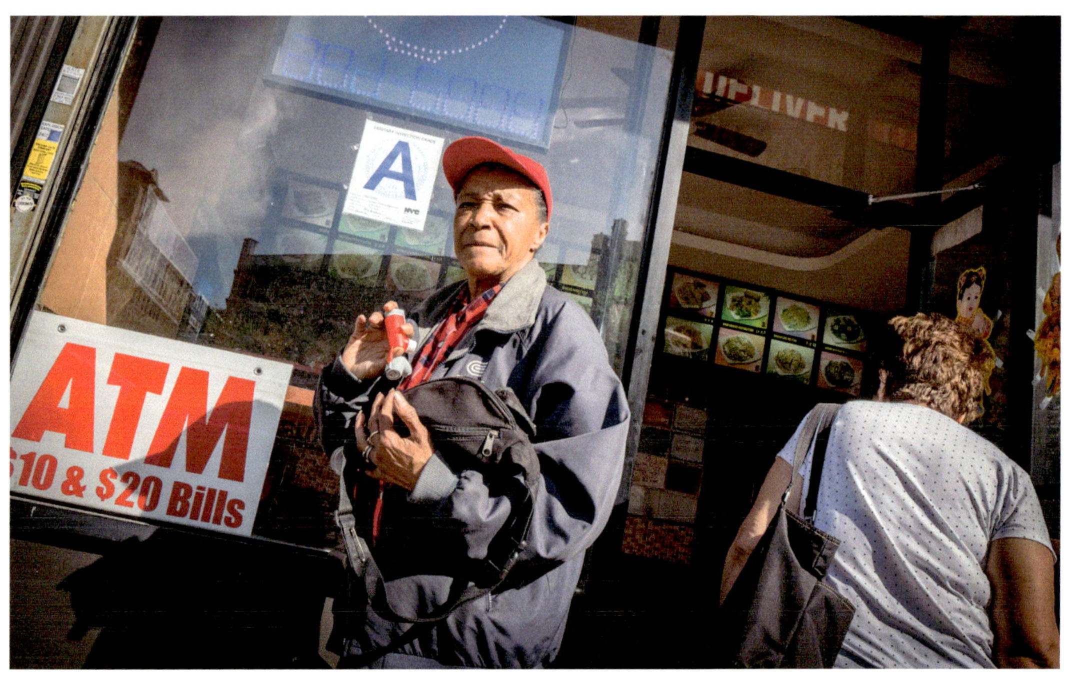

Woman with an inhaler.

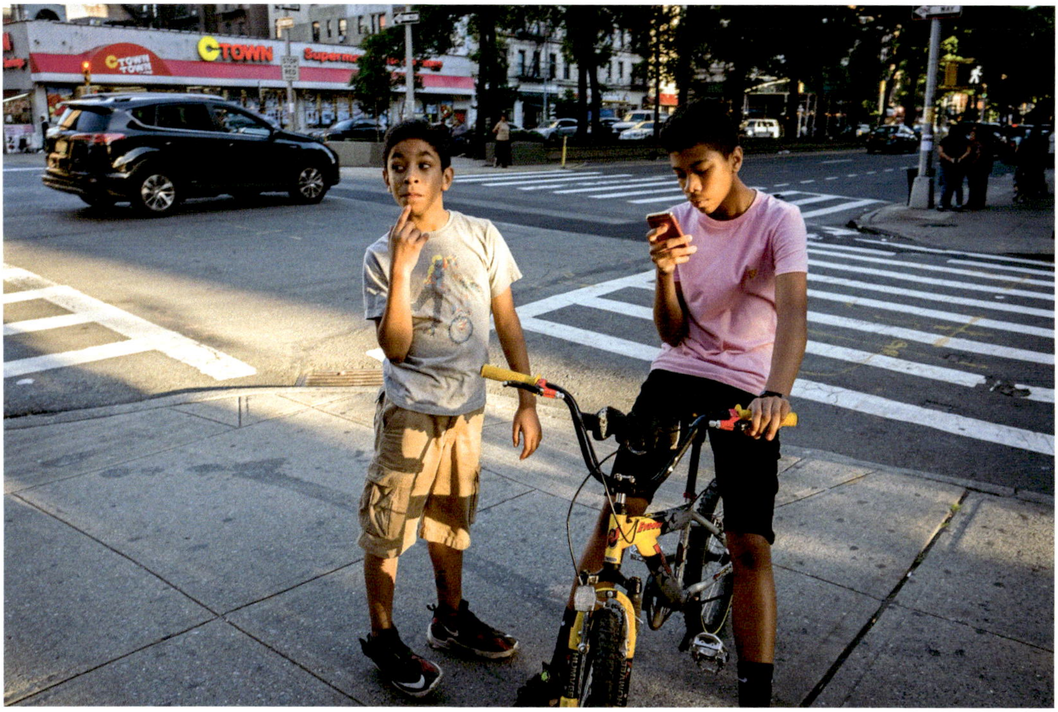

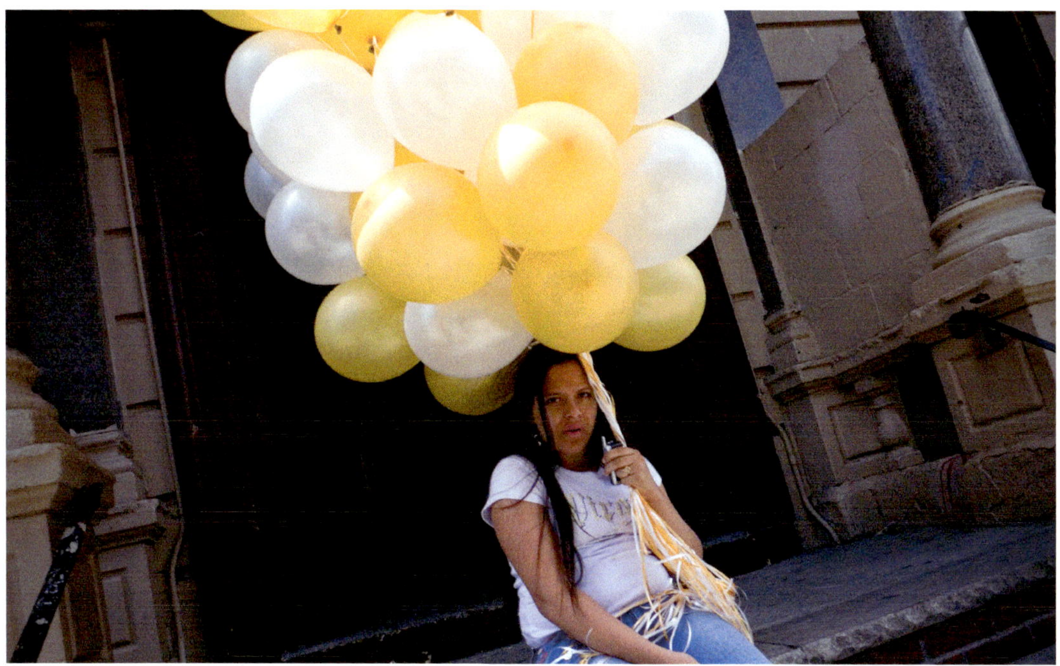

Two boys.

Girl with birthday balloons.

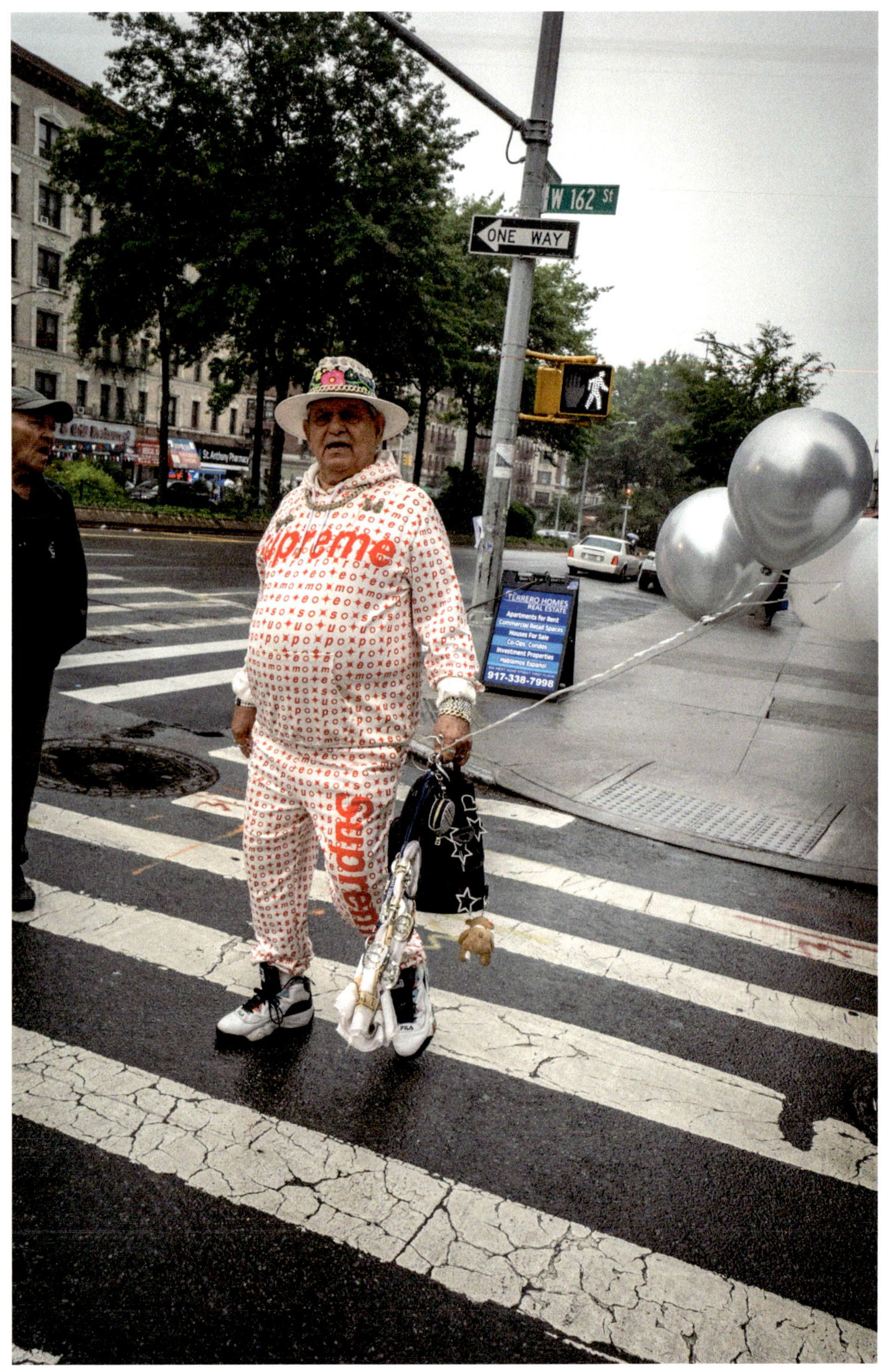

Man wearing "Supreme" clothing, an influential manufacturer of streetwear.

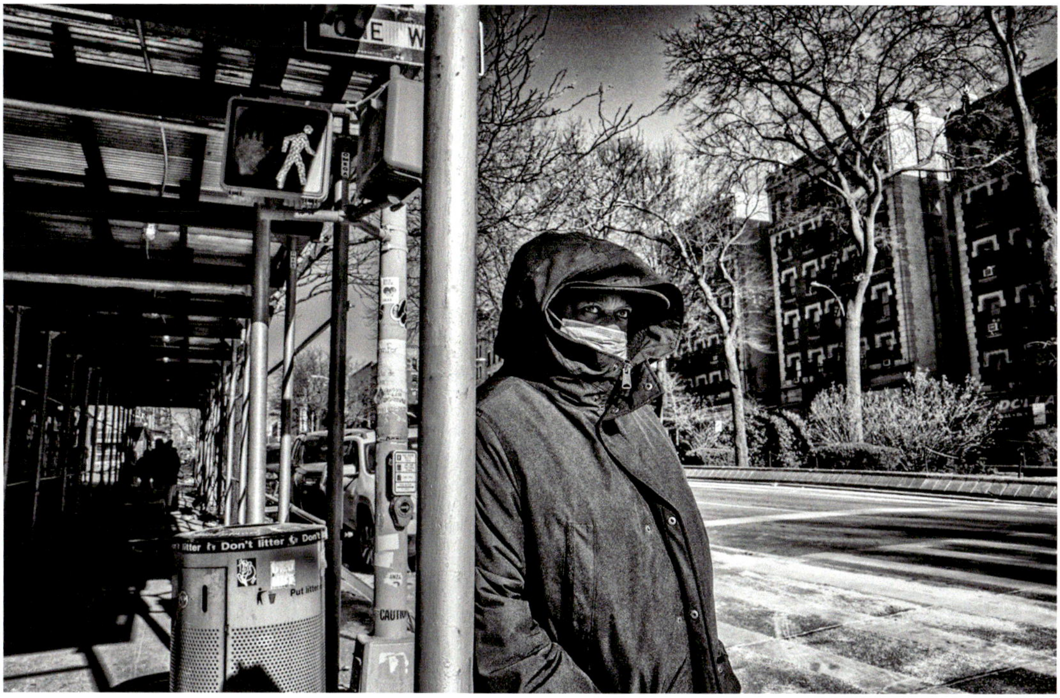

Bundled up against the chill of winter.

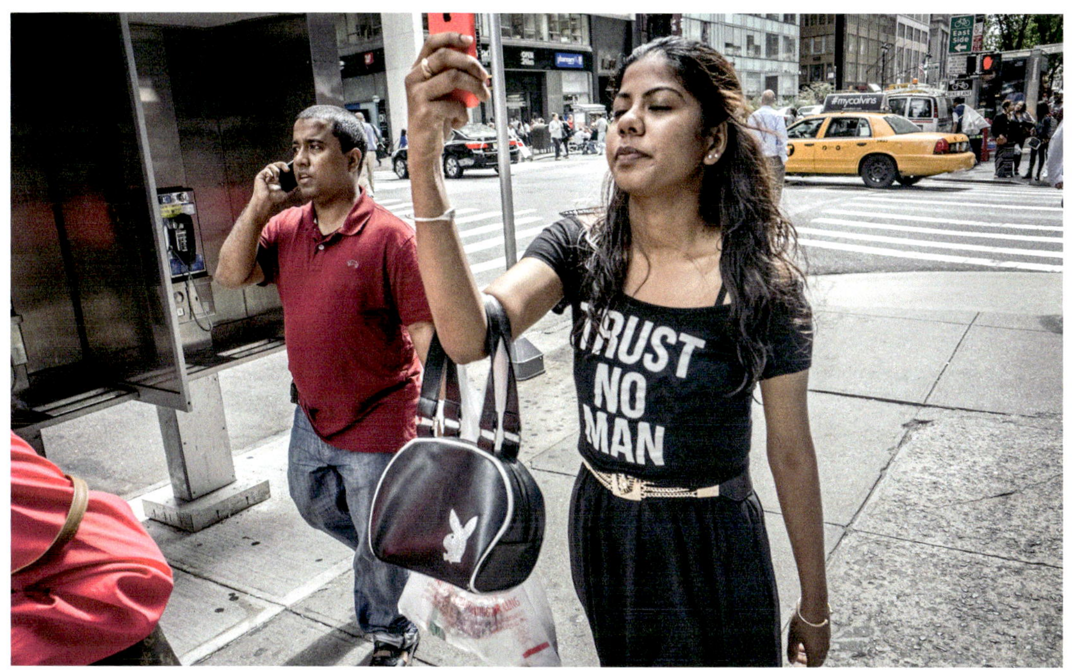

A young woman takes a selfie. She wears a t-shirt that says, "Trust No Man."

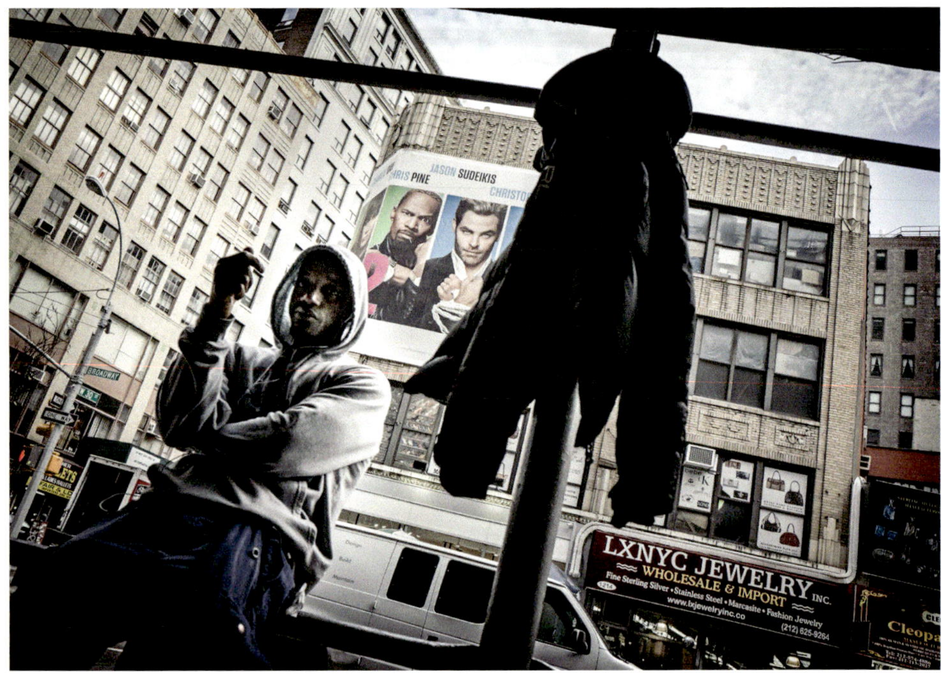

In many neighborhoods along Broadway, men just "hang out"—either on a break from work or looking for a "deal."

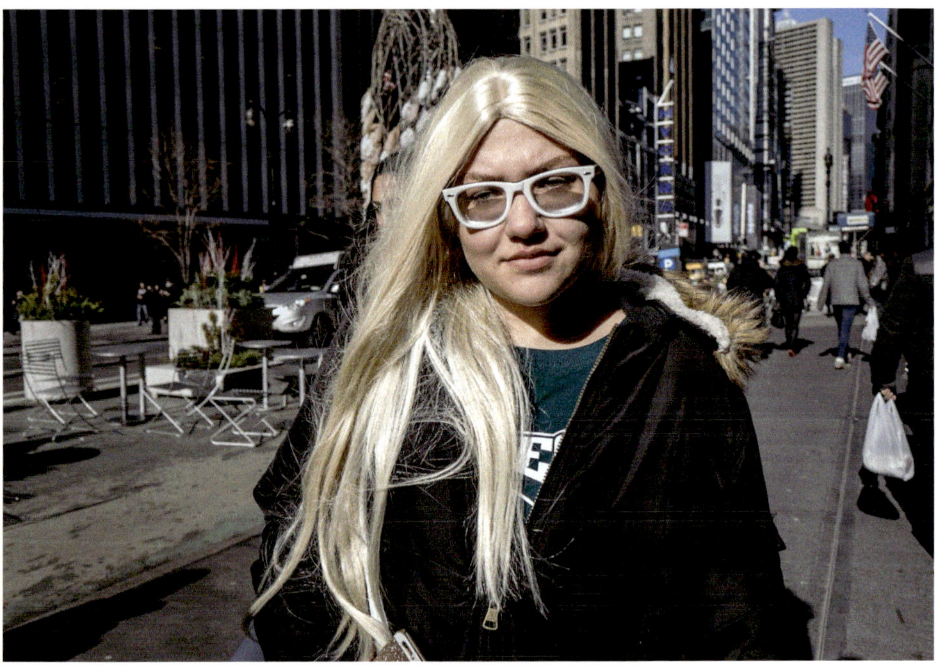

Portrait of a woman wearing fashionable glasses.

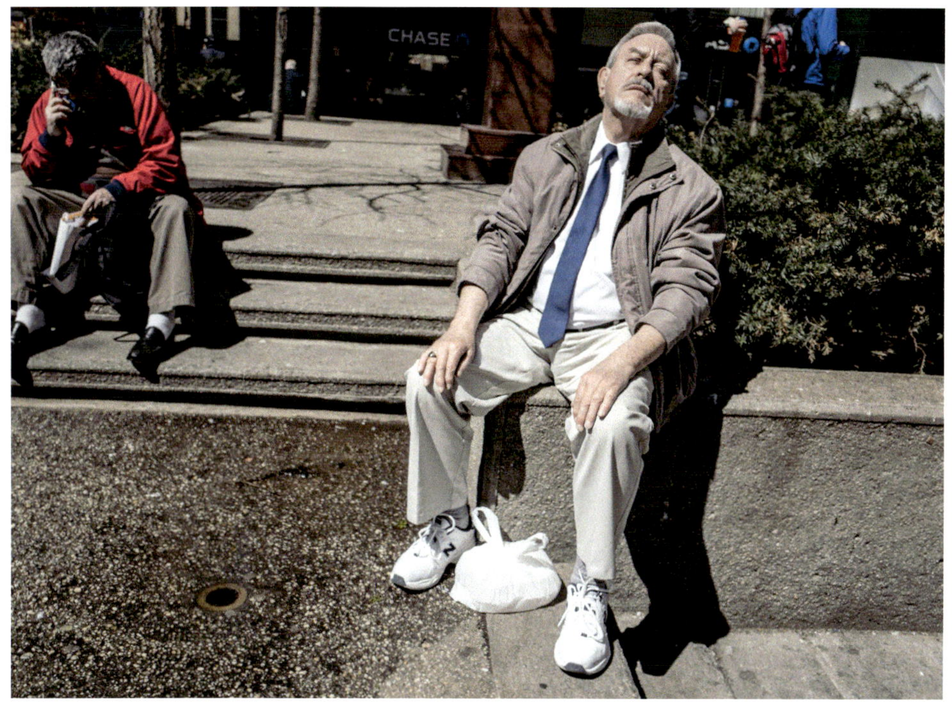

Man catches some sun during his lunch break.

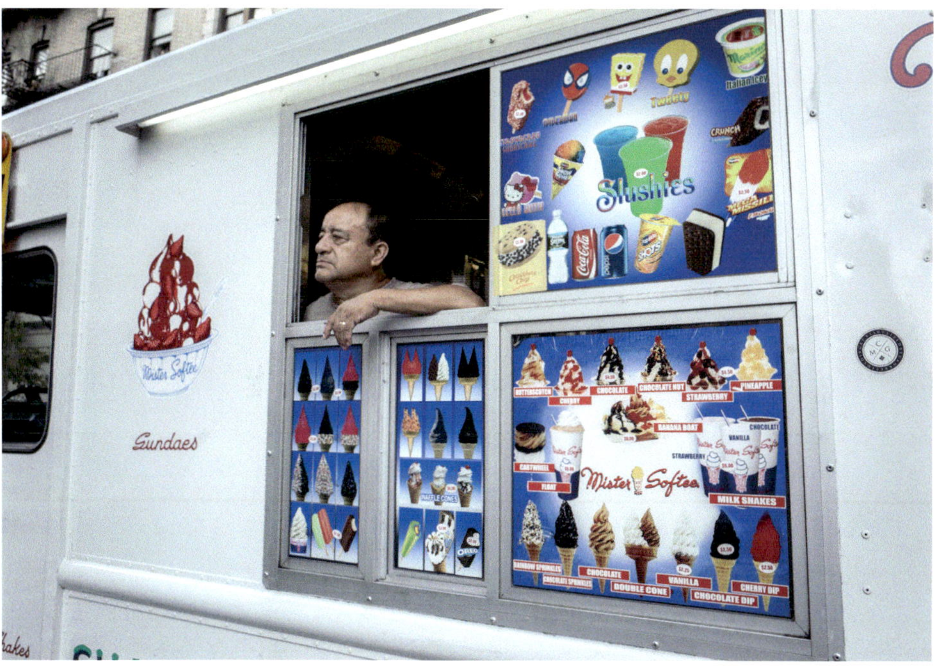

An ice cream vendor in his truck.

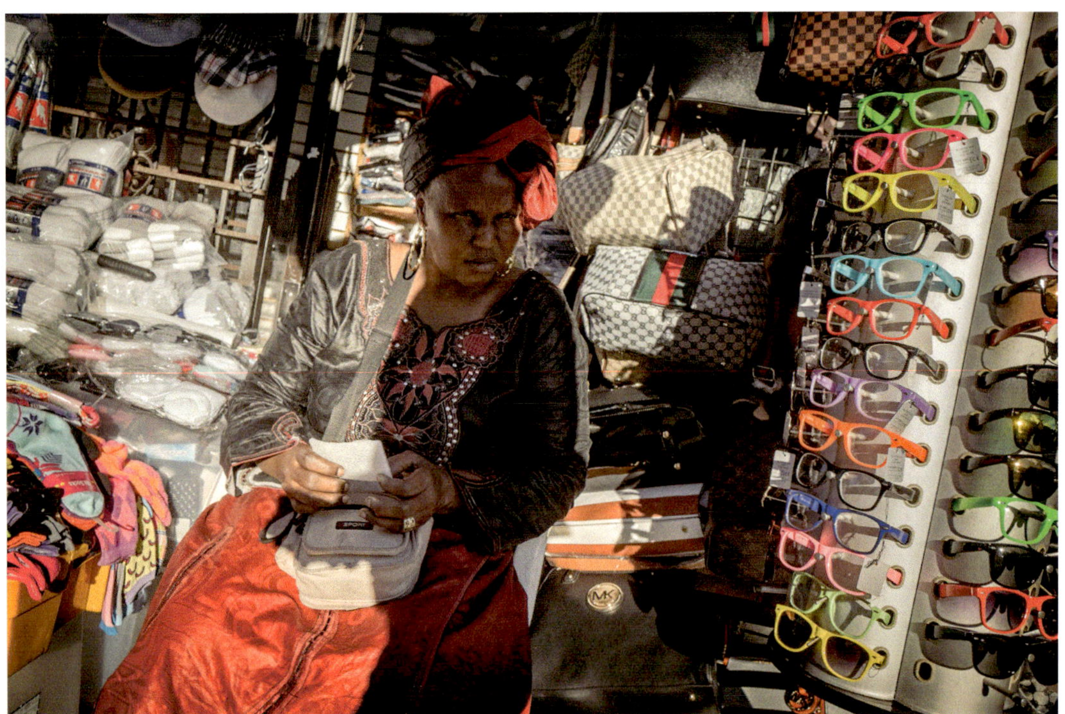

A vendor in her stall.

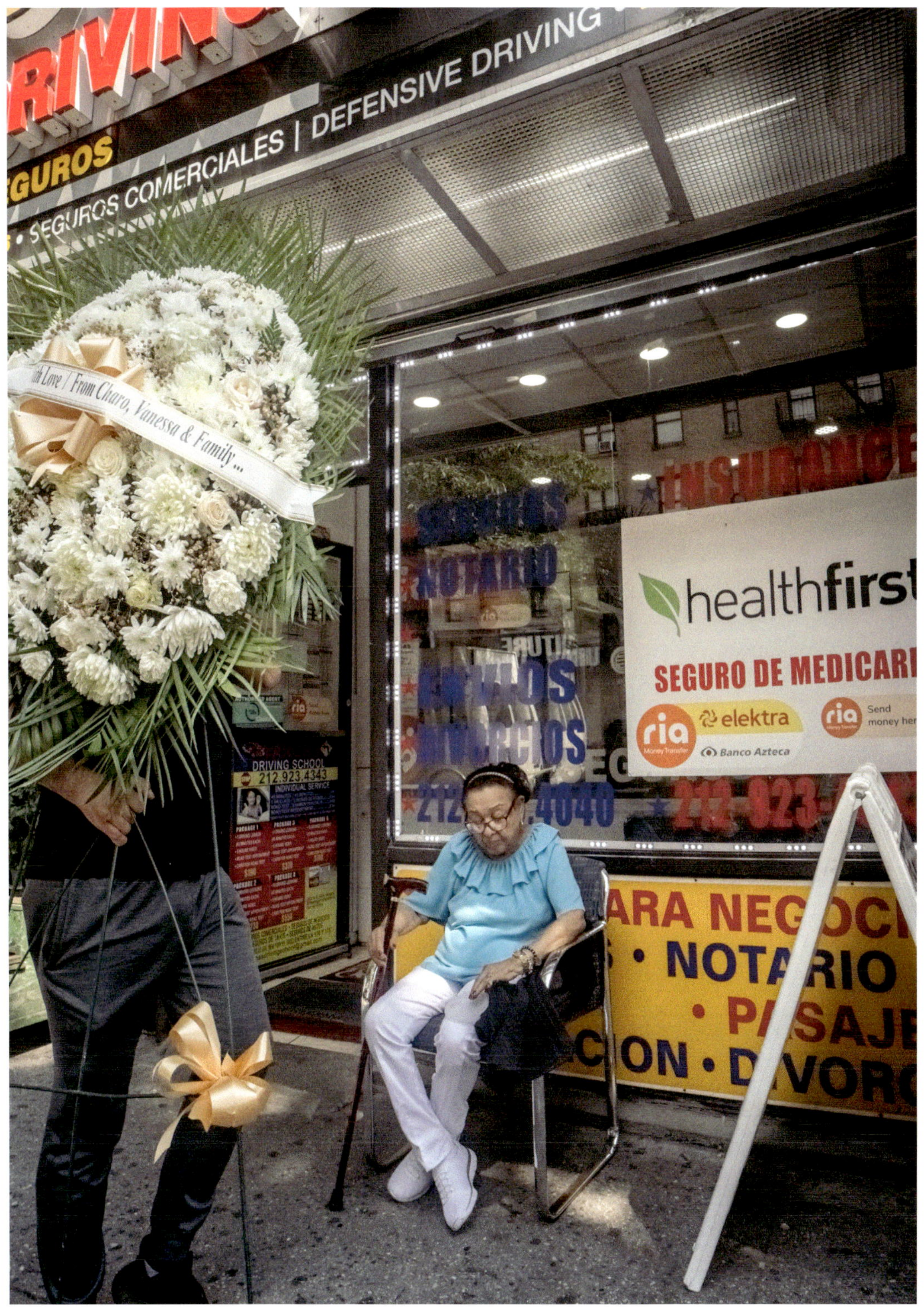
DRIVING
SEGUROS
SEGUROS COMERCIALES | DEFENSIVE DRIVING
With Love / From Charo, Vanessa & Family...
INSURANCE
healthfirst
SEGURO DE MEDICARE
ria Money Transfer
elektra
Banco Azteca
ria Send money here
SERVICIOS NOTARIO
DRIVING SCHOOL
212.923.4343
INDIVIDUAL SERVICE
ARA NEGOCI
NOTARIO
PASAJE
CION • DIVORC

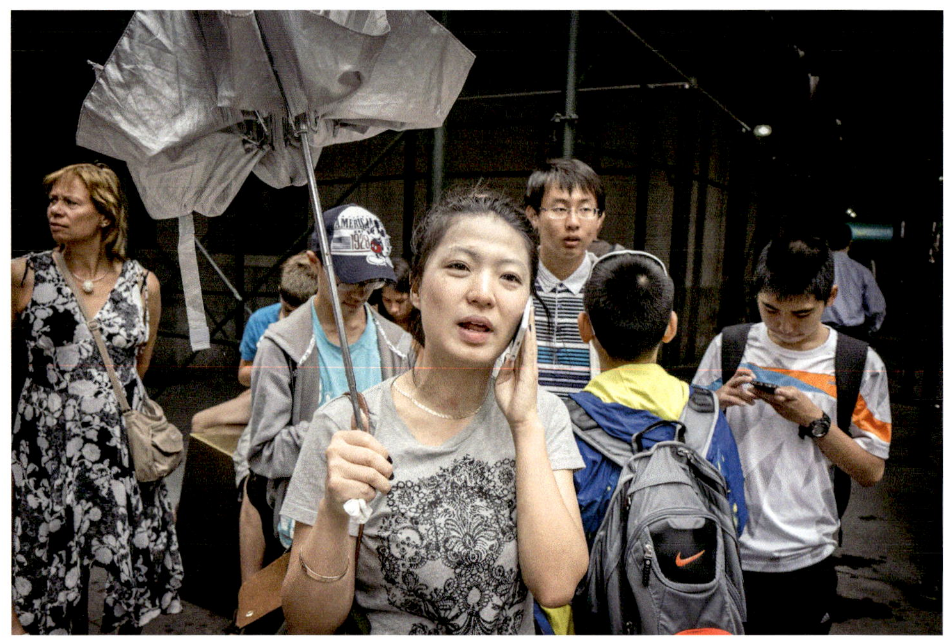

A tour guide leads a group of tourists.

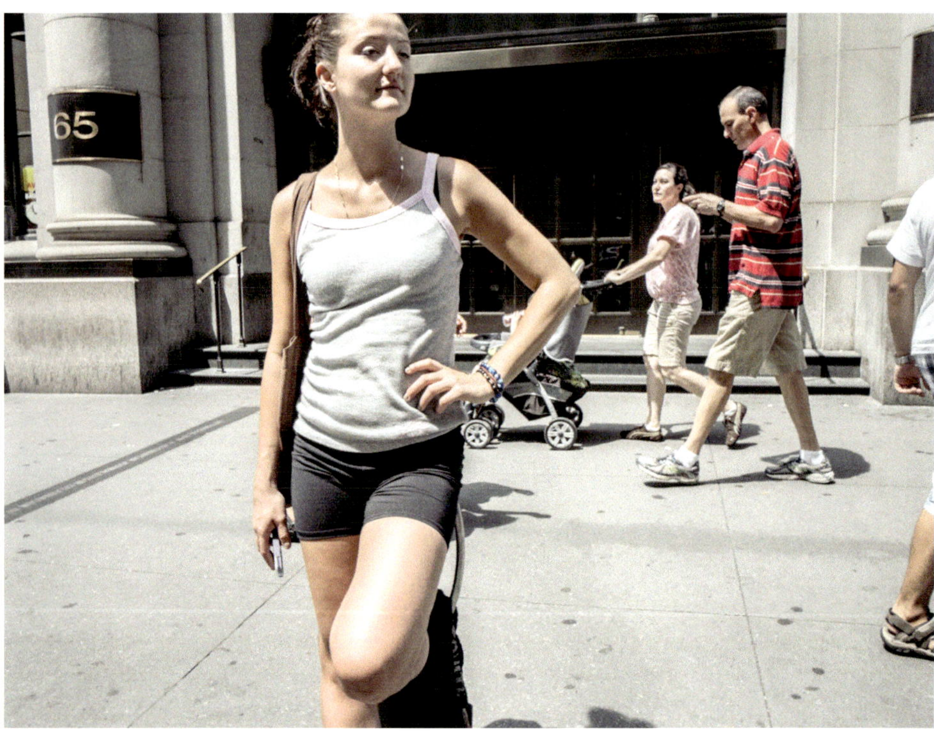

A young woman strikes a pose amid the motion of urban life.

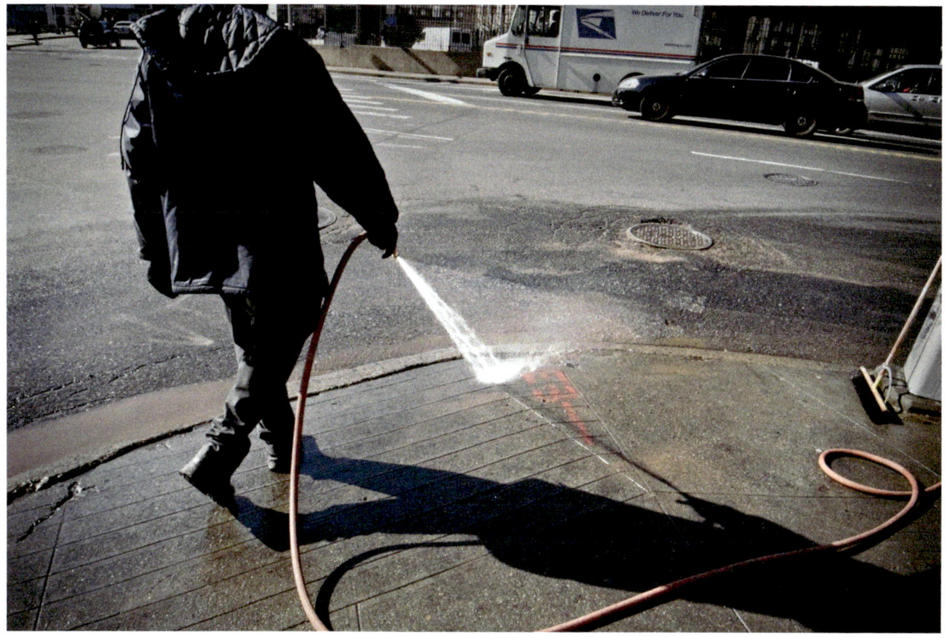

Keeping the sidewalk clean in front of his shop, a man hoses it down.

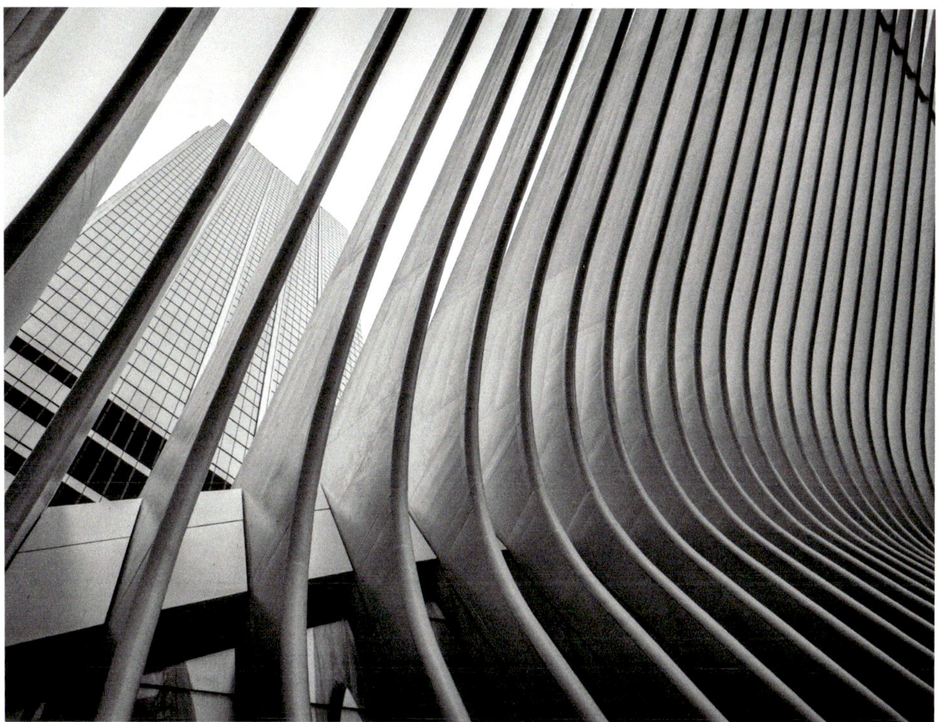

The Oculus is a transportation hub of twelve subway lines and a PATH station.

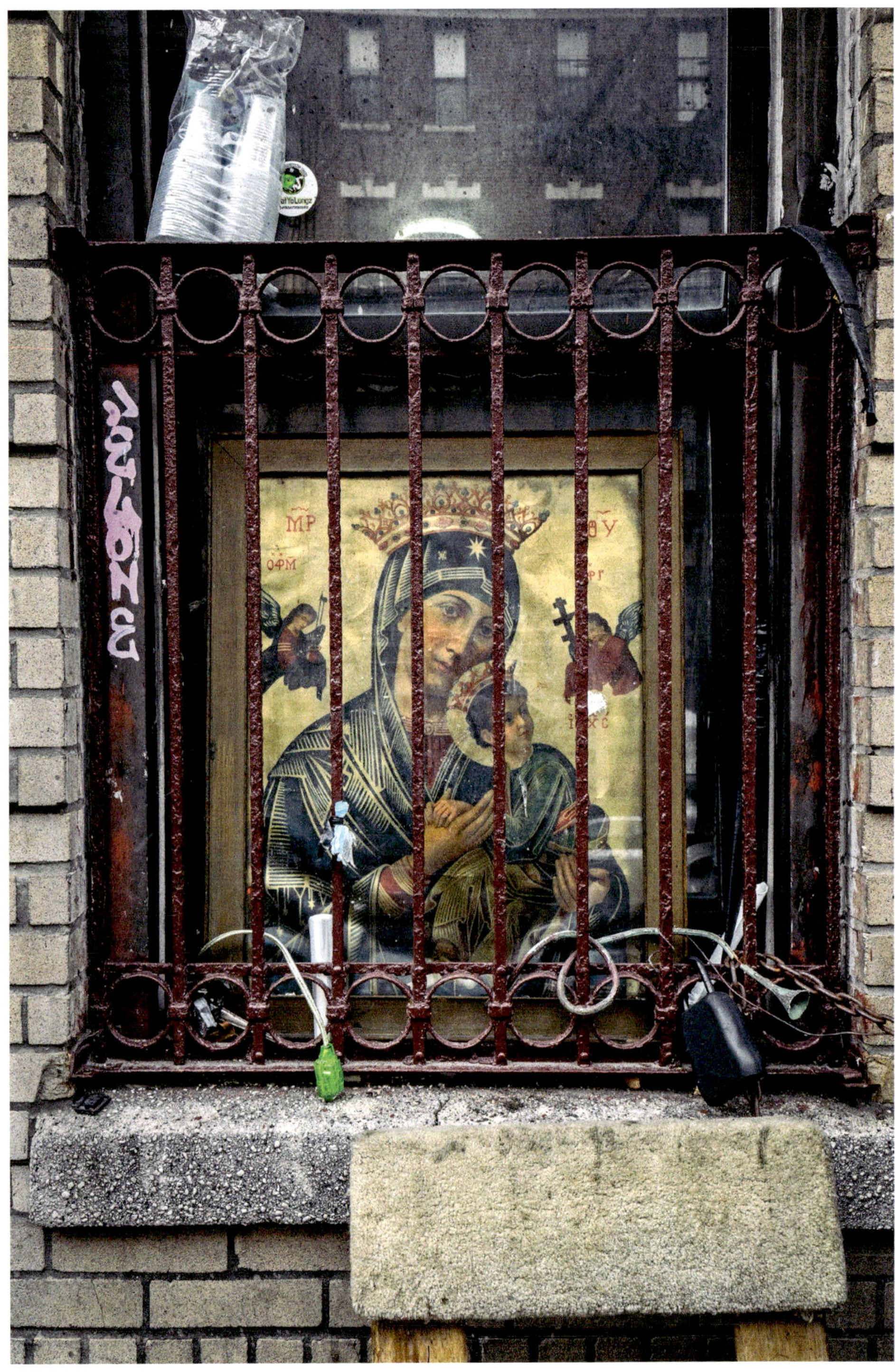

A sacred painting of Mary and Jesus rests behind weathered iron bars, blending faith and urban grit on a city street.

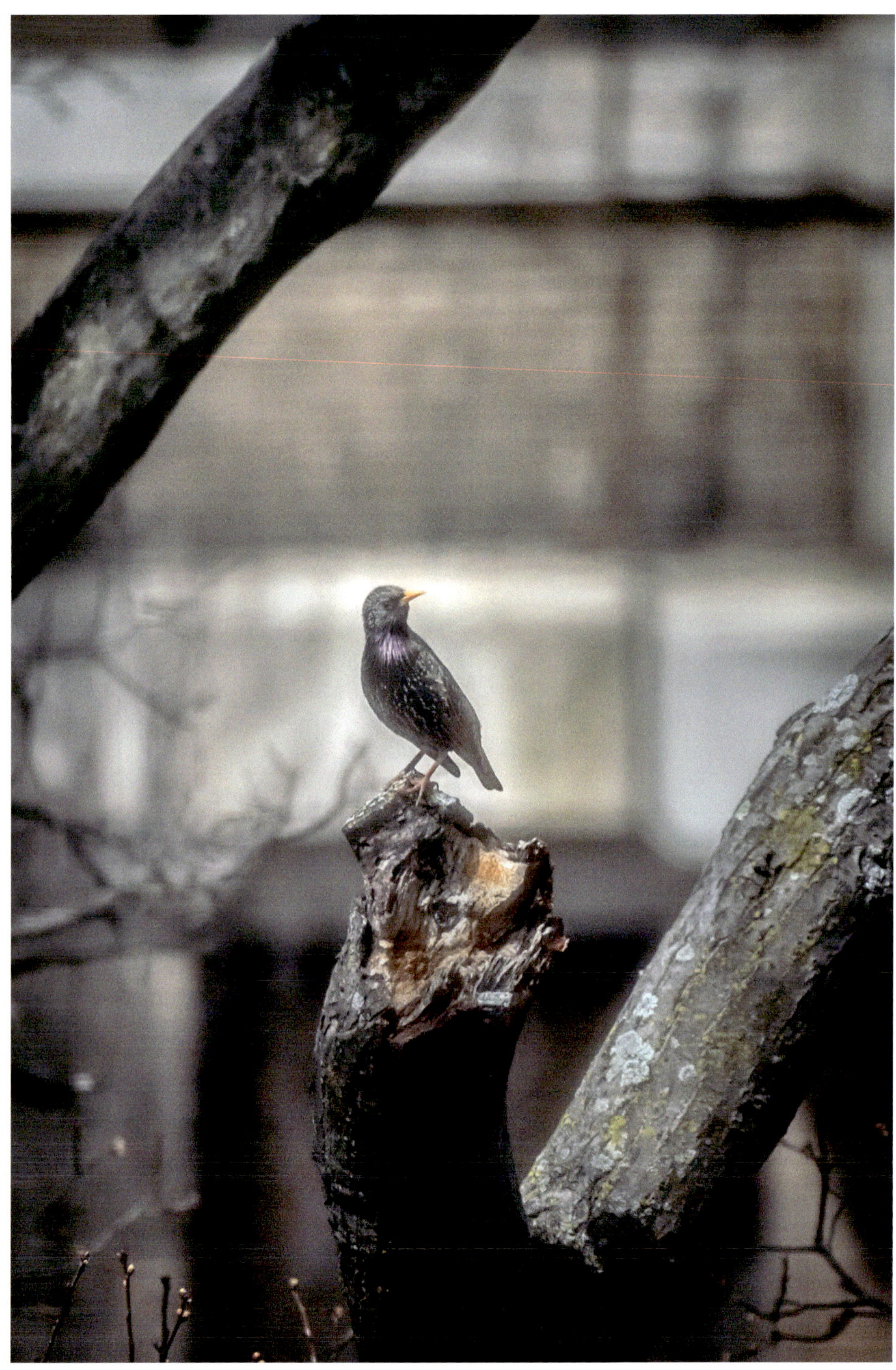

Despite claims to the contrary, New York does have wildlife. Here a starling perches on a tree stump on a traffic island on Broadway.

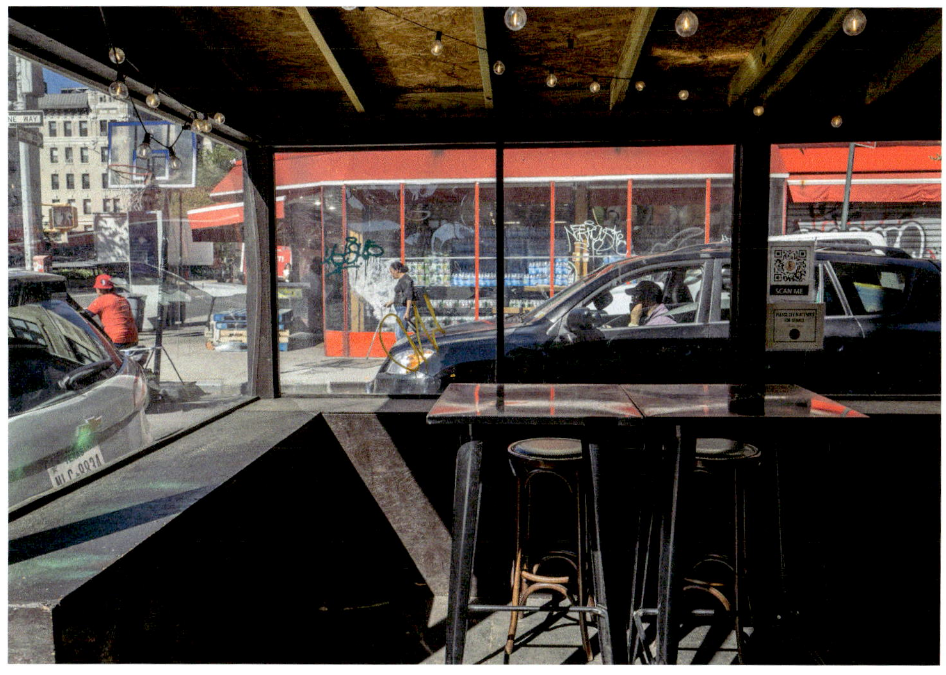

A dining shed. These were quite prevalent in the city during COVID.

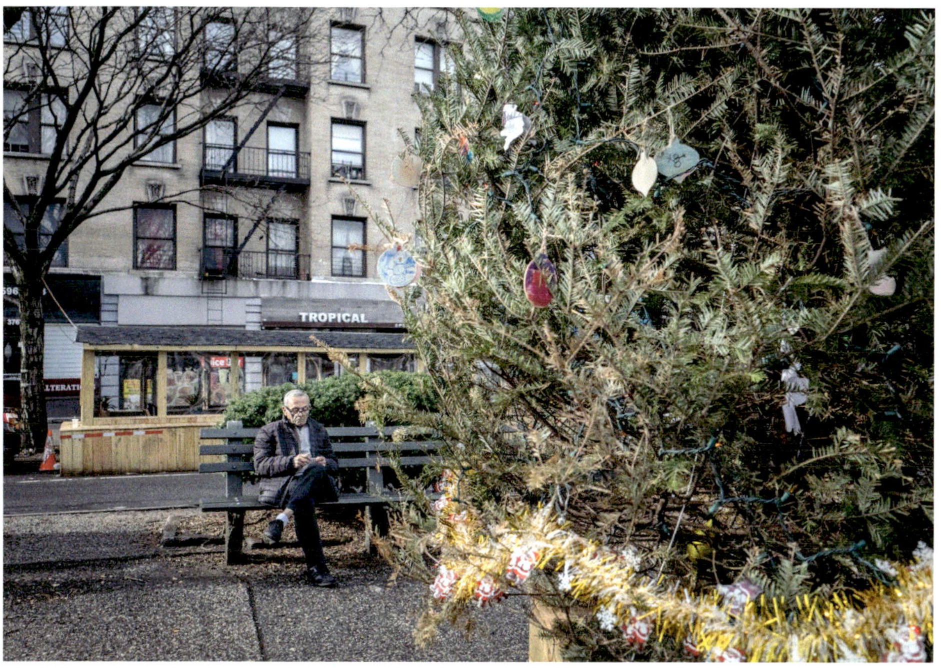

Ilka Tanya Payan Park. Ilka Tanya Payan was a Dominican-born actress and a HIV/AIDS activist.

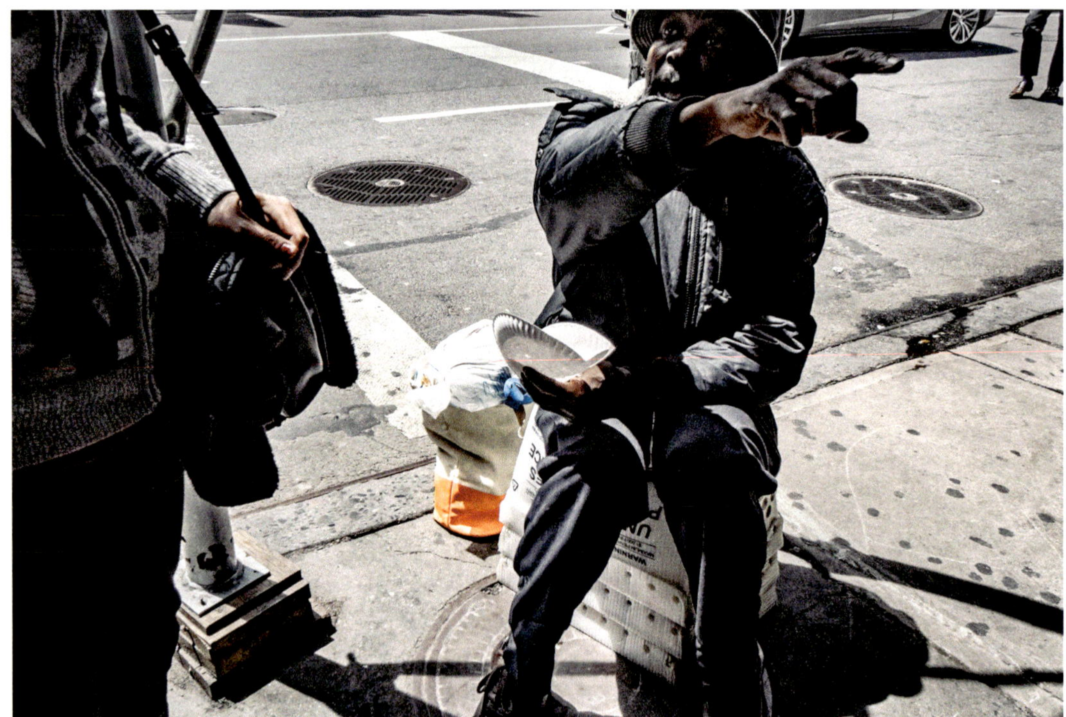

Giving directions.

Opposite page: A face of a poster peers through a weathered window of a dining shed.

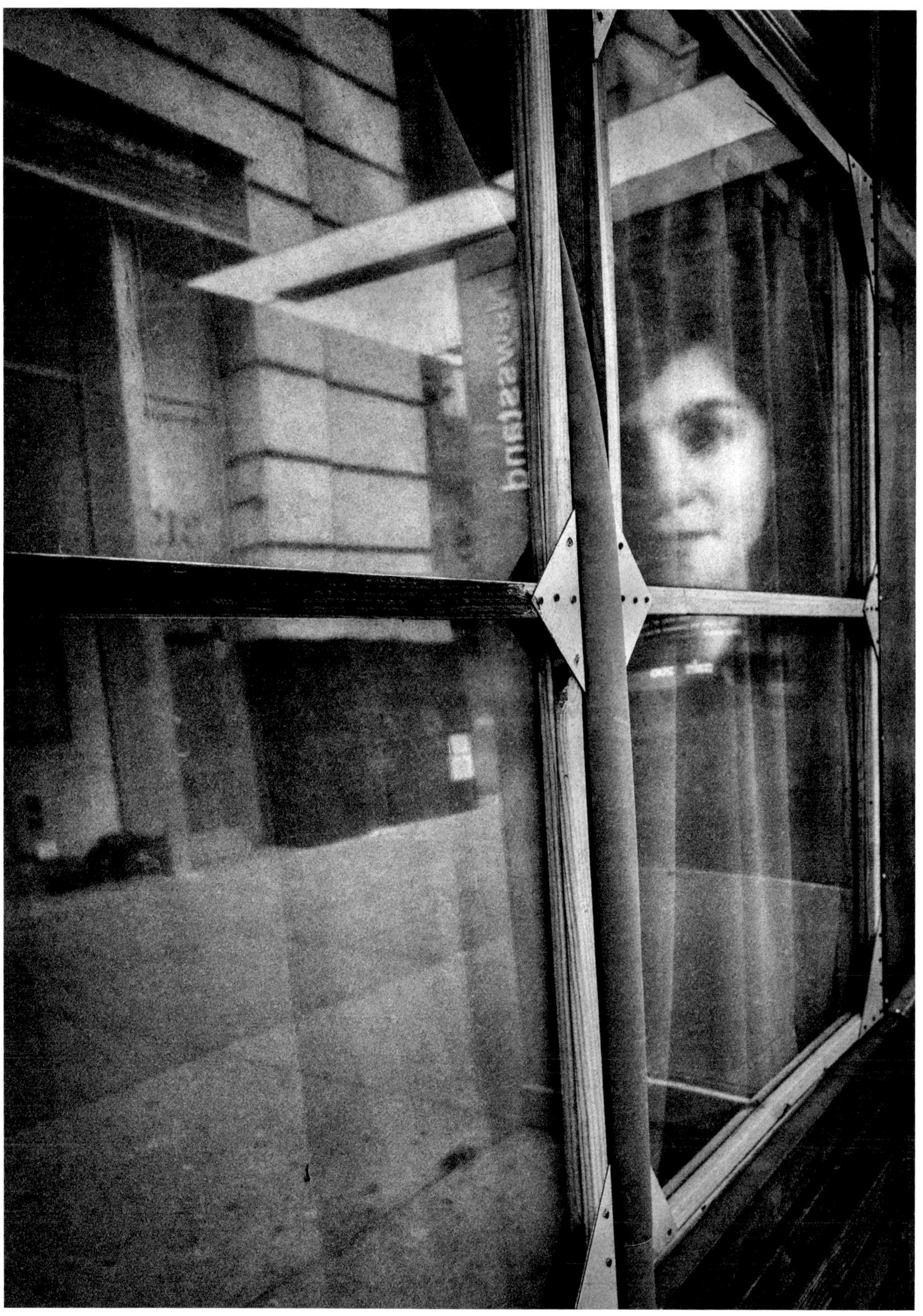

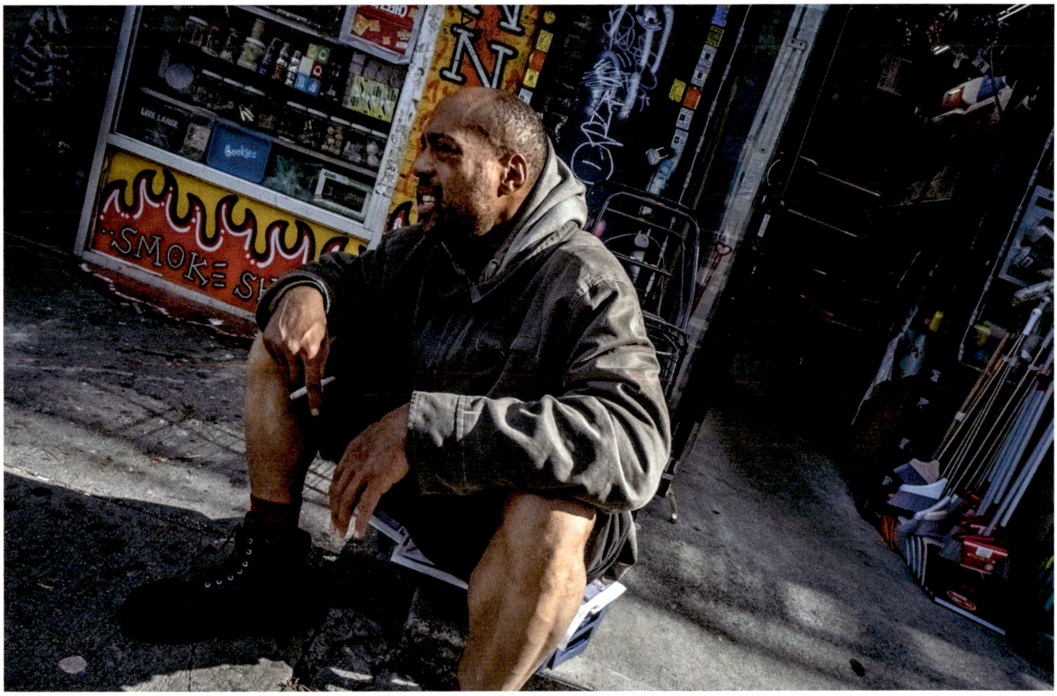

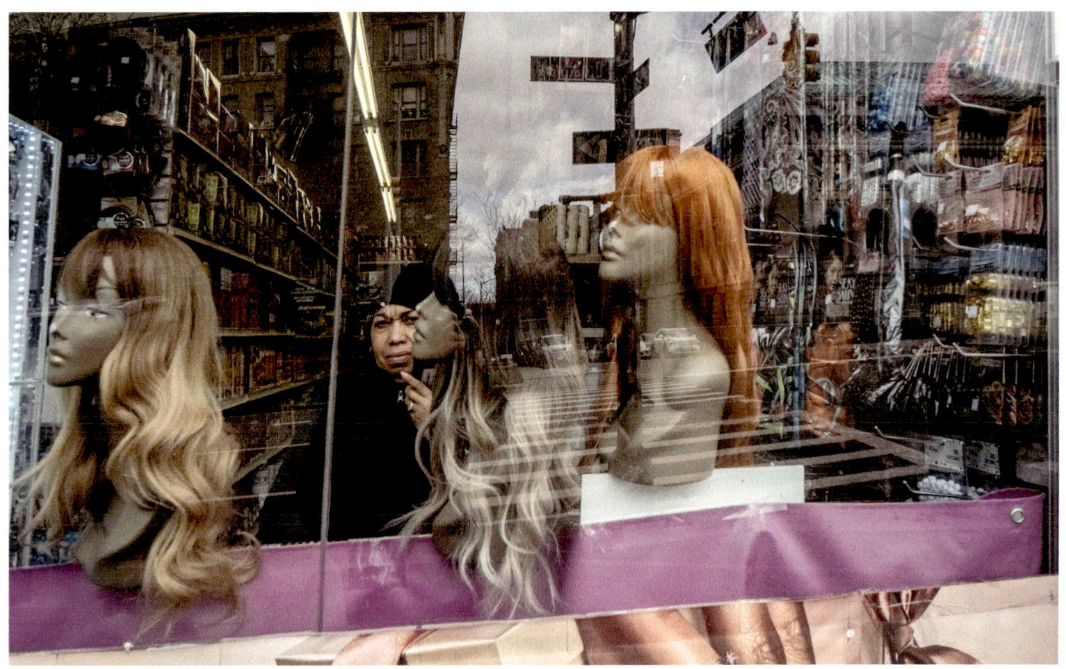

Having a cigarette in front of a smoke shop.

A woman looks out of a window of a beauty supply shop.

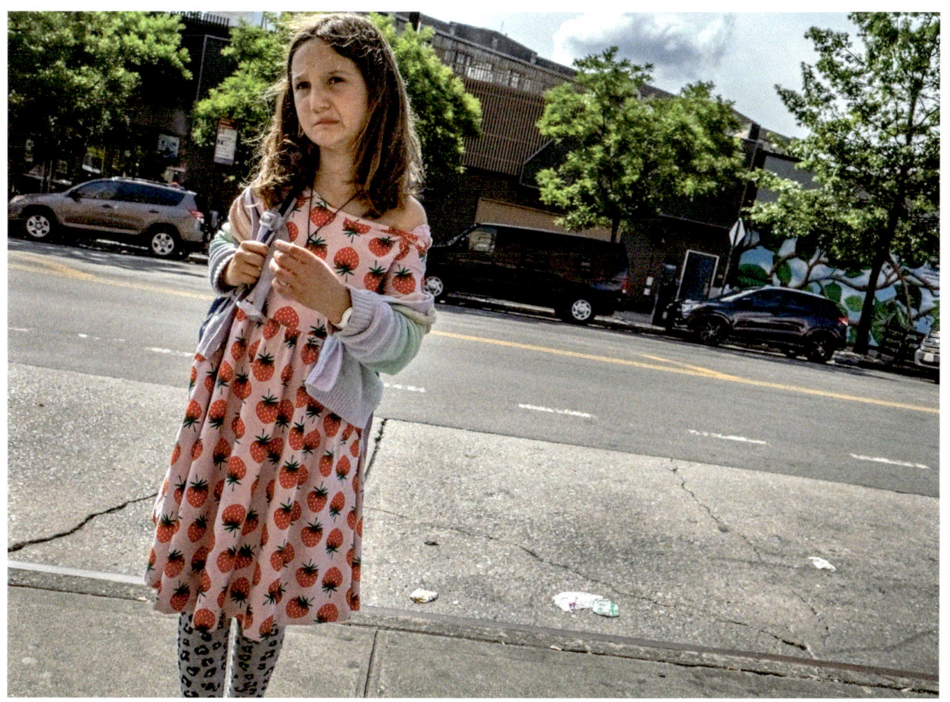

Face of disgust.

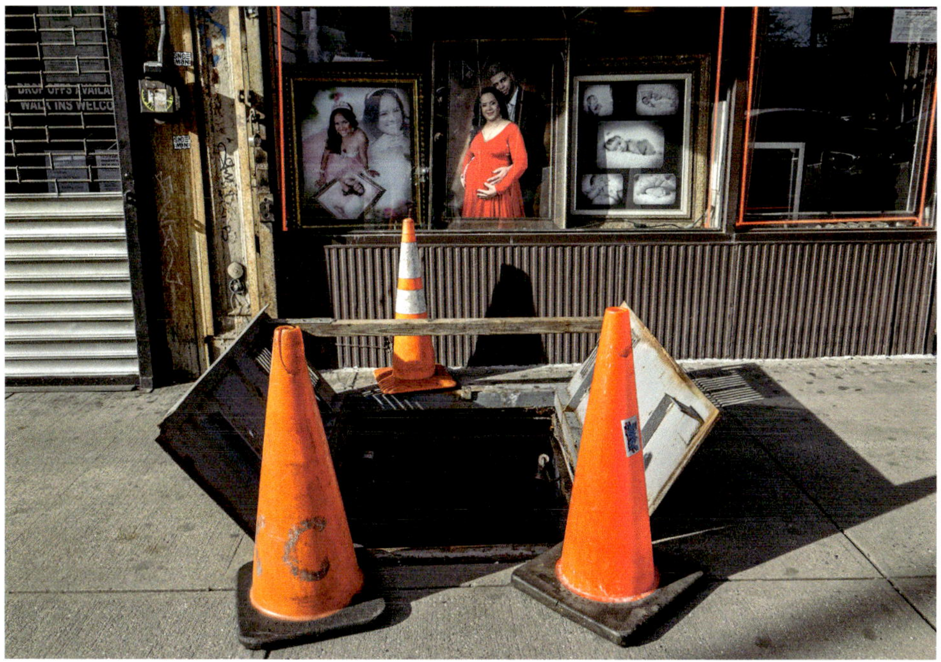

A trio of cones outside a photo studio.

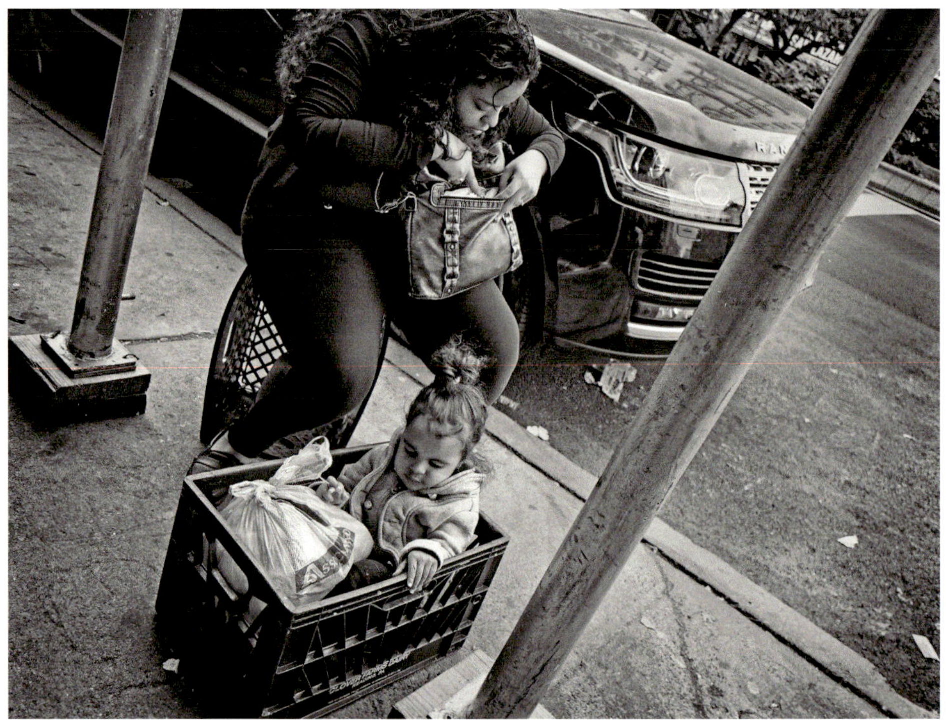

A woman searches through her purse while her child is placed in a milk crate for safe keeping.

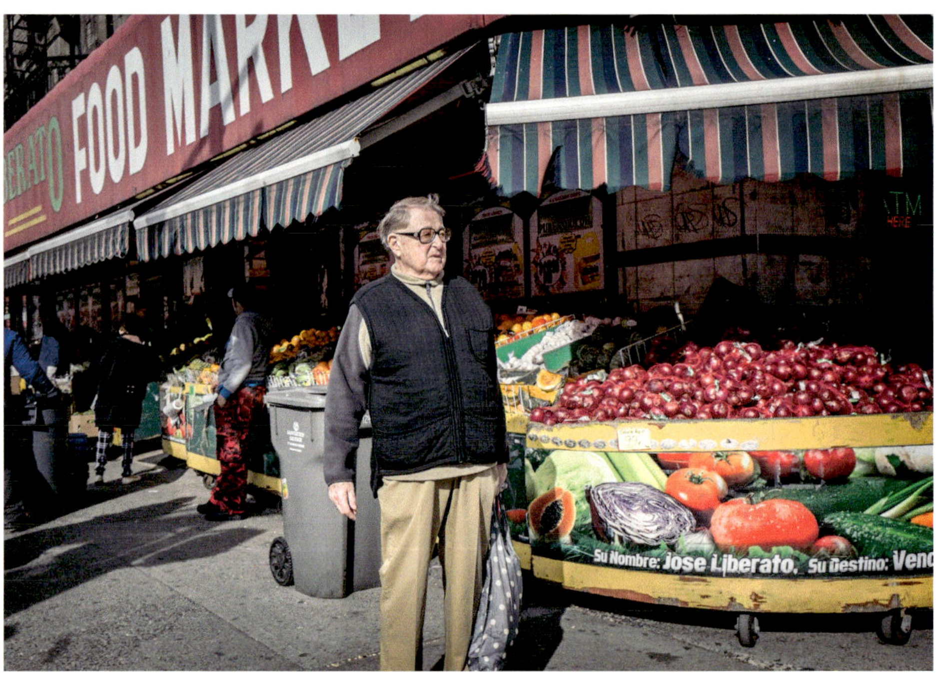

Outside a food market, a man stares down Broadway.

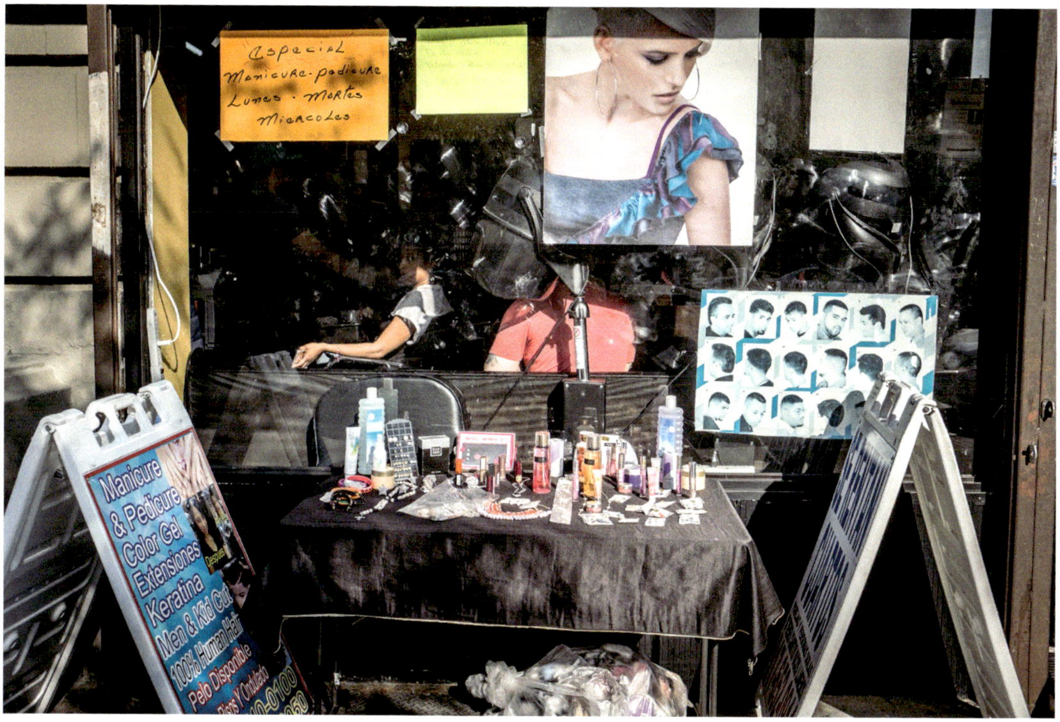

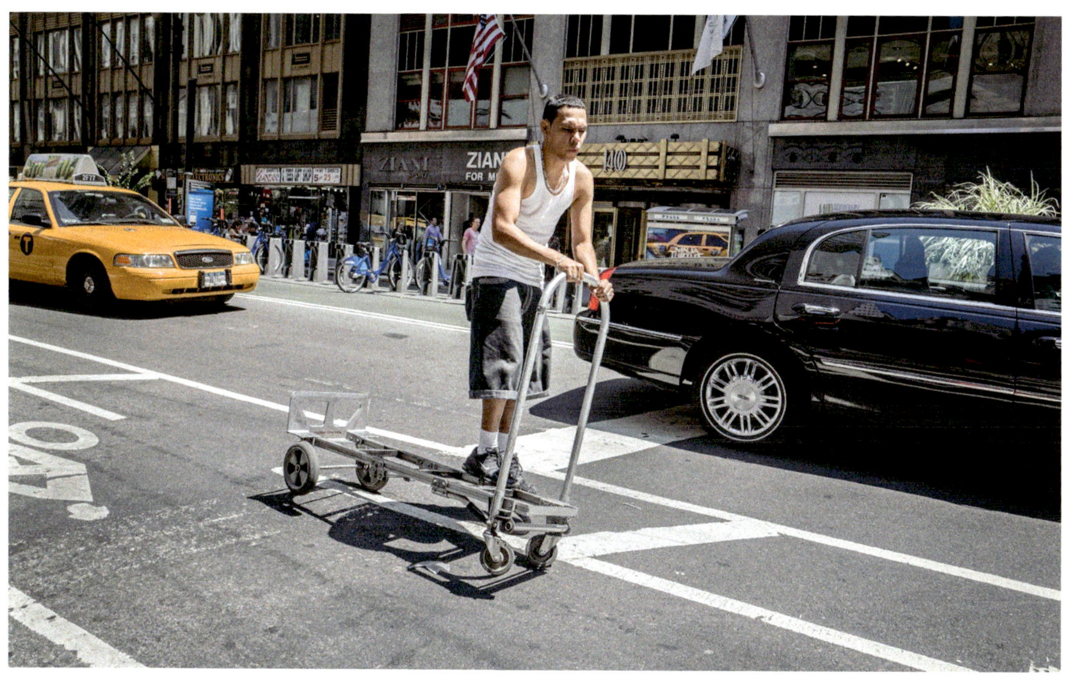

Items for sale on a table outside a beauty shop.

Skating down Broadway on a handcart.

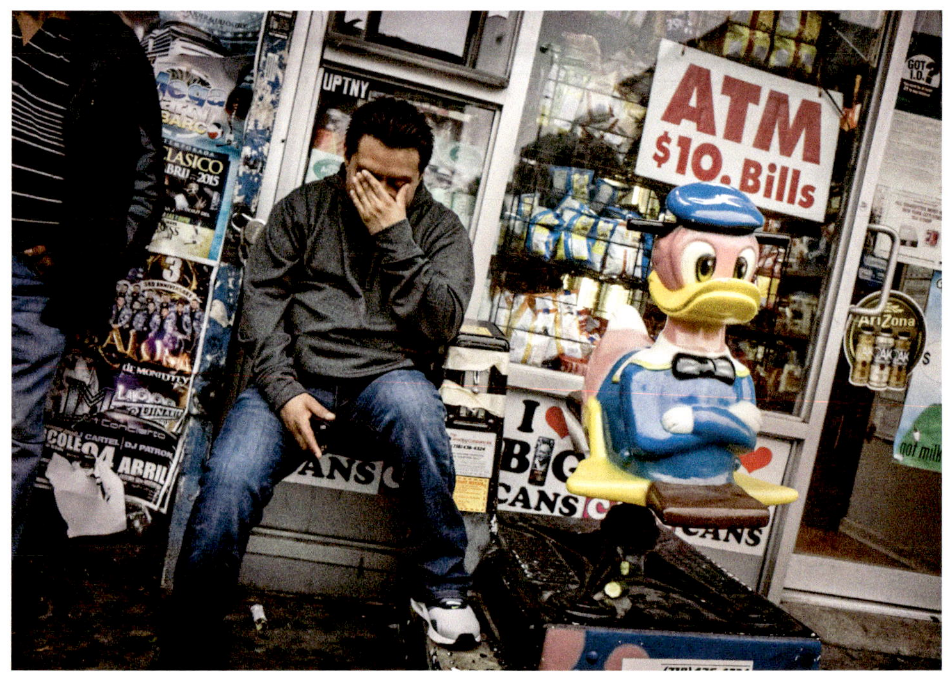

Outside a bodega.

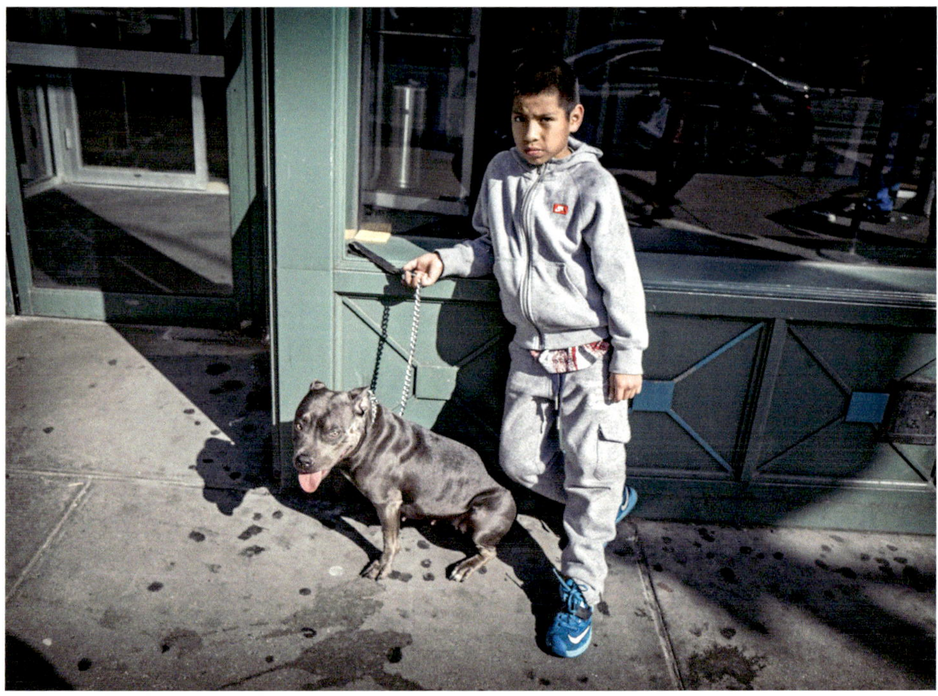

A boy and his dog outside a bank.

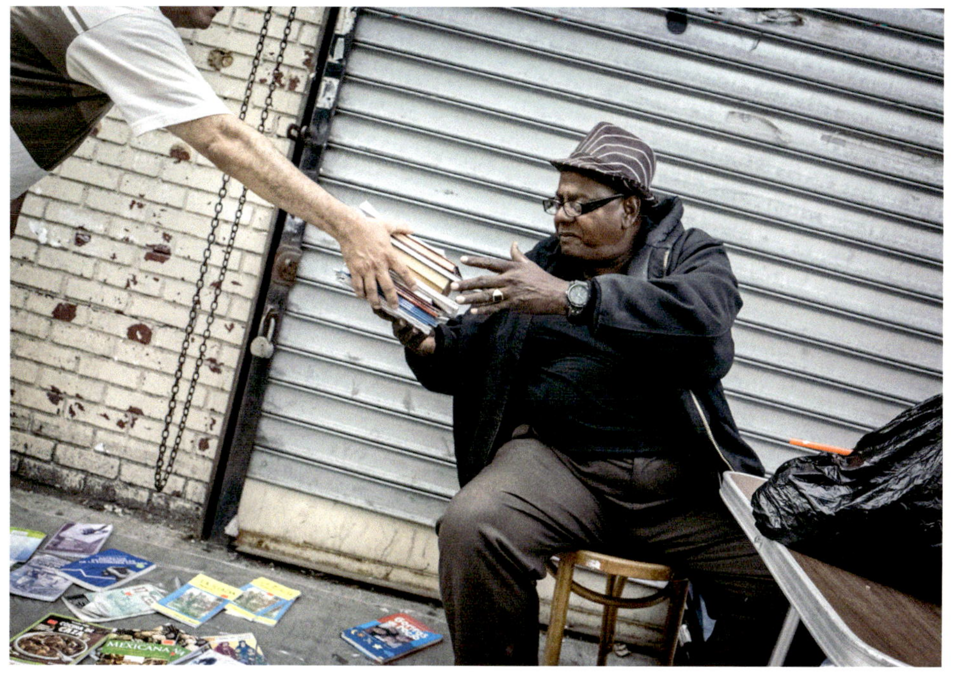

A bookseller is handed a handful of books to sell.

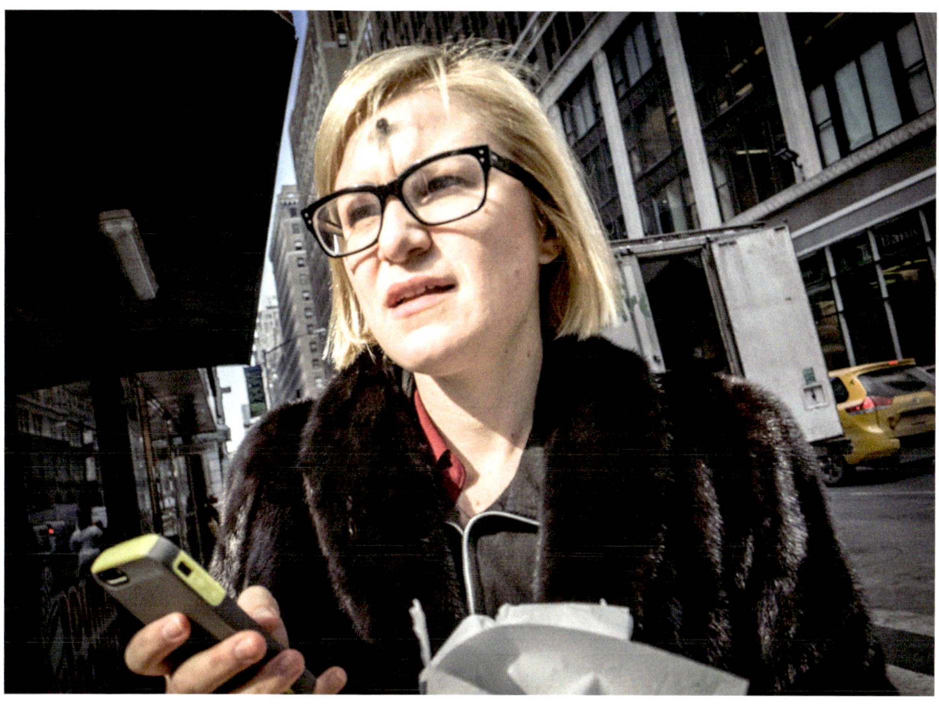

Ash Wednesday.

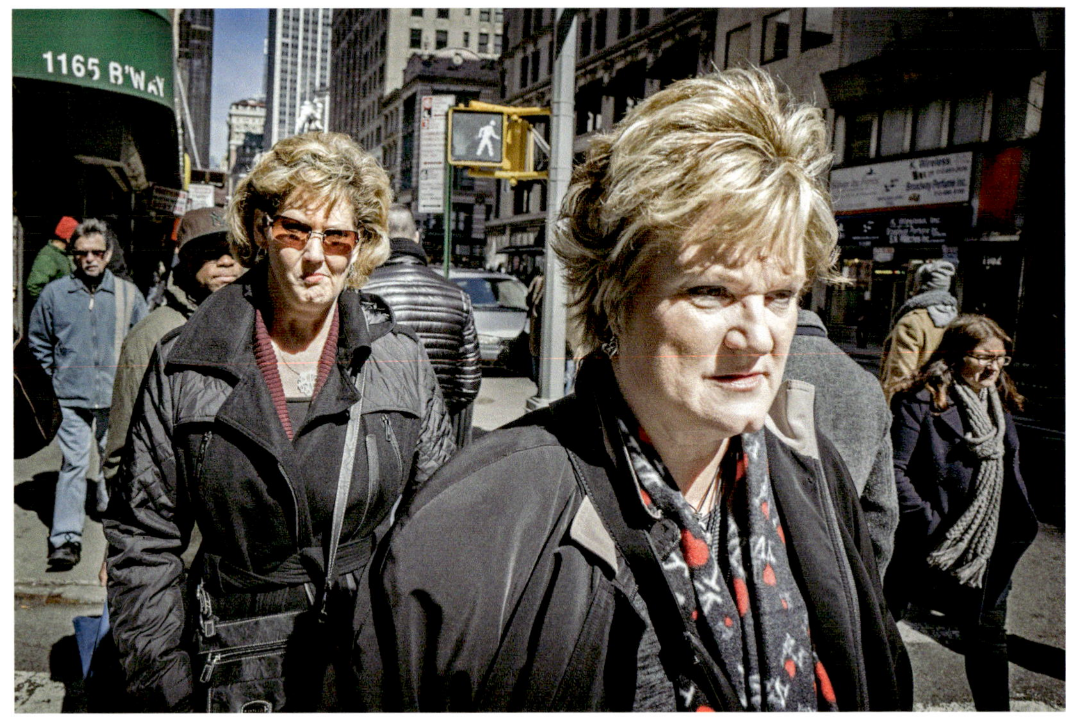

Determined faces navigate the streets, each carrying their own story.

Opposite page: Bundled against the cold, a man holds a placard and advertisement for a wig shop.

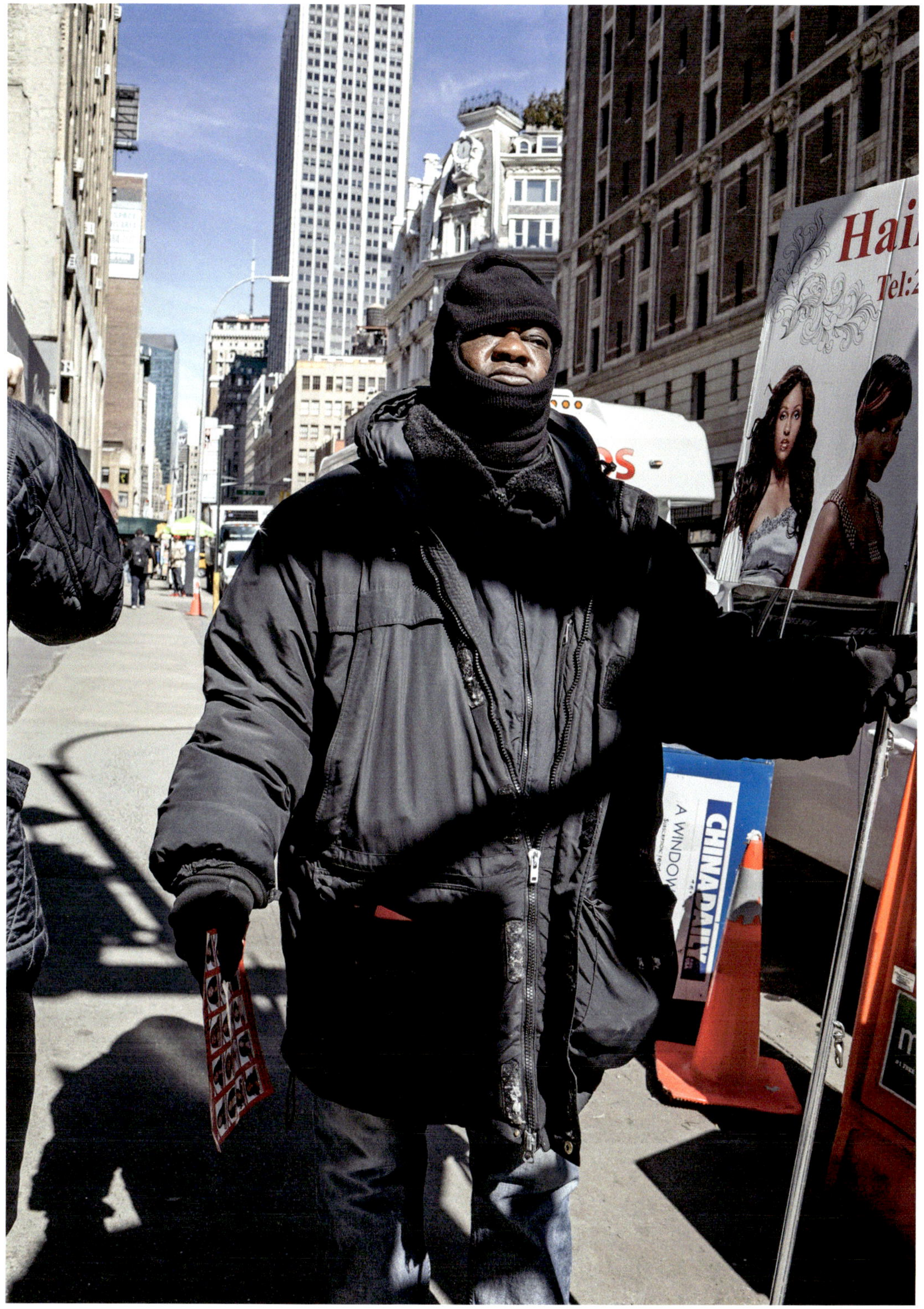
Hai
Tel:2
CHINA DAILY
A WINDOW

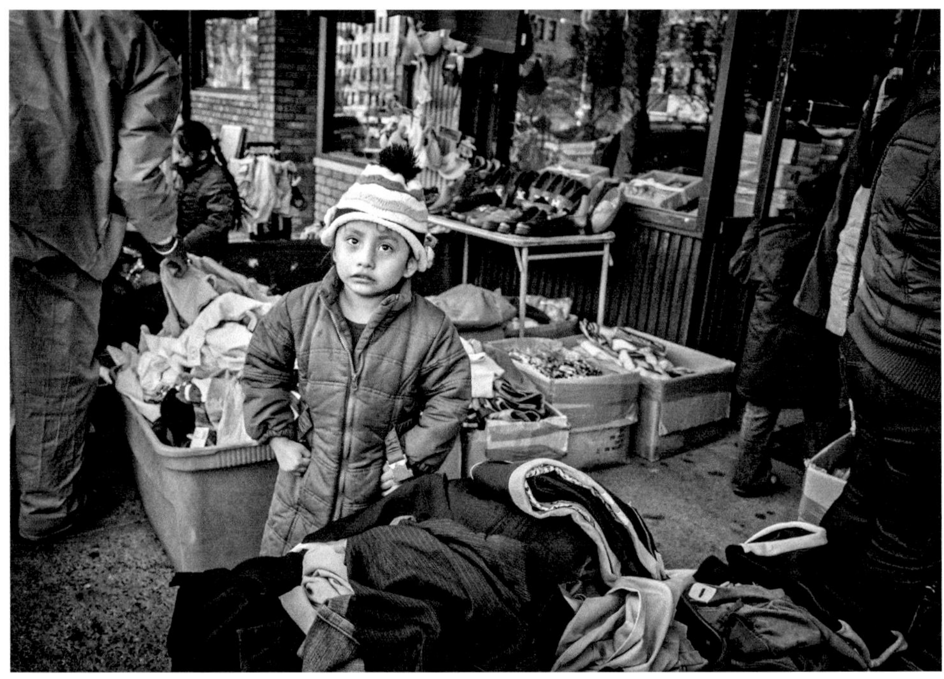

Amid the hustle of a street market, a young child stands quietly, her curious gaze capturing a moment of stillness.

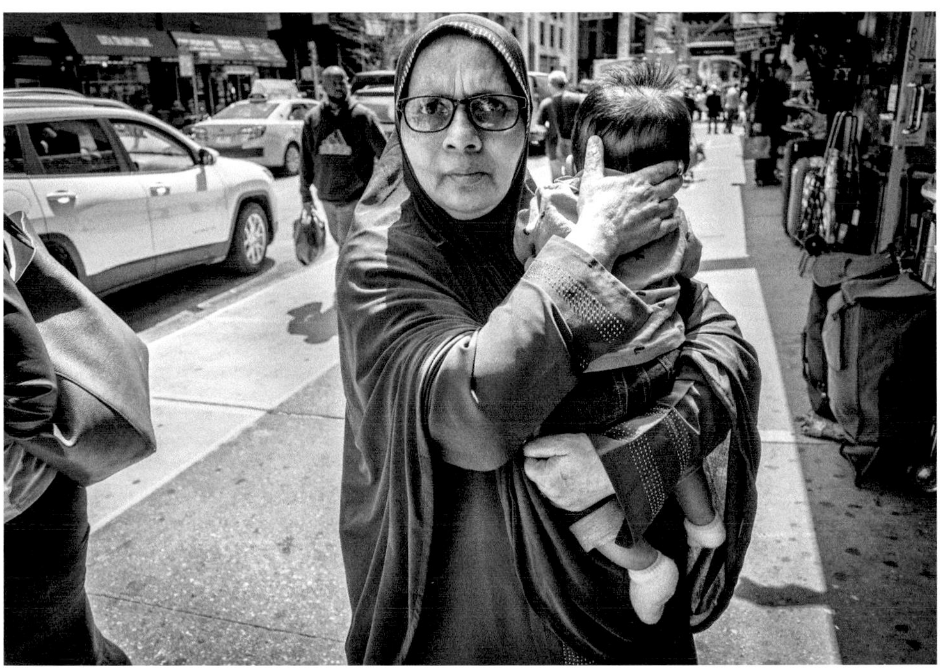

A grandmother shields her grandchild from the distractions of the street.

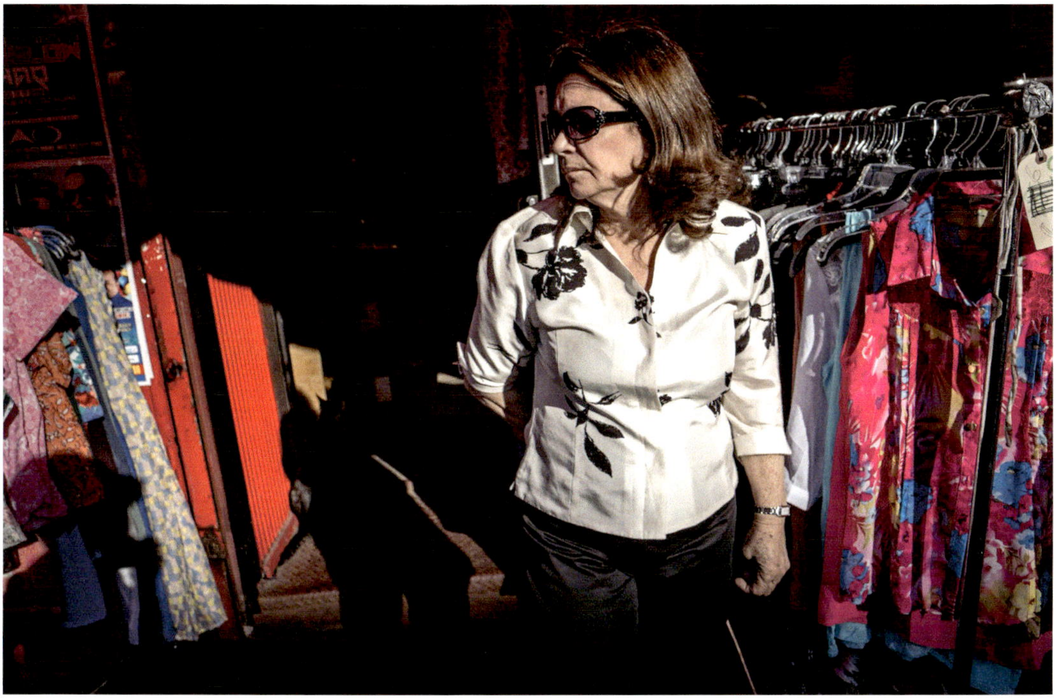

A clothing vendor outside her shop.

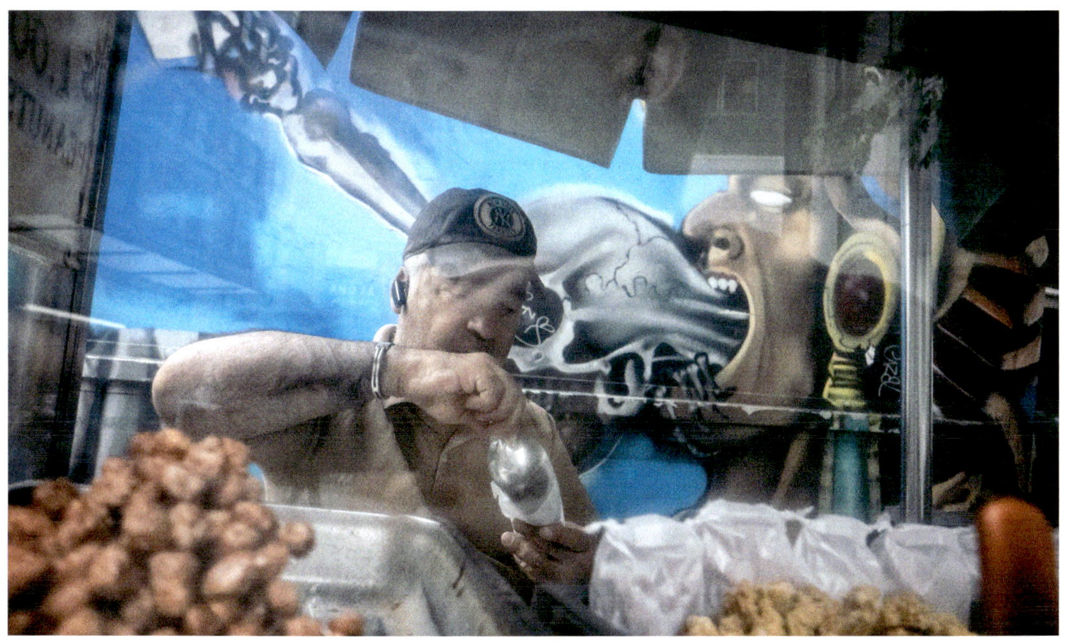

Through a street vendor's cart window, he carefully serves a portion of nuts framed by vibrant graffiti that tells its own urban story.

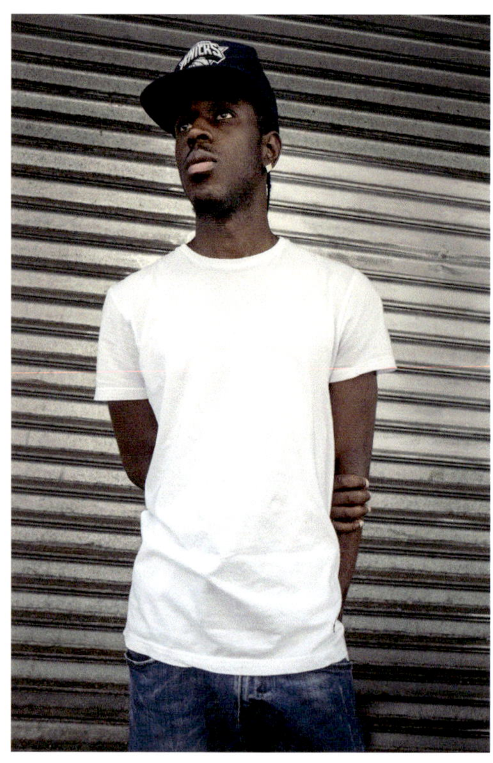

Left: Poised and thoughtful, a young man stands against a metal gate backdrop.

Below: A man shares a laugh as he converses on the phone.

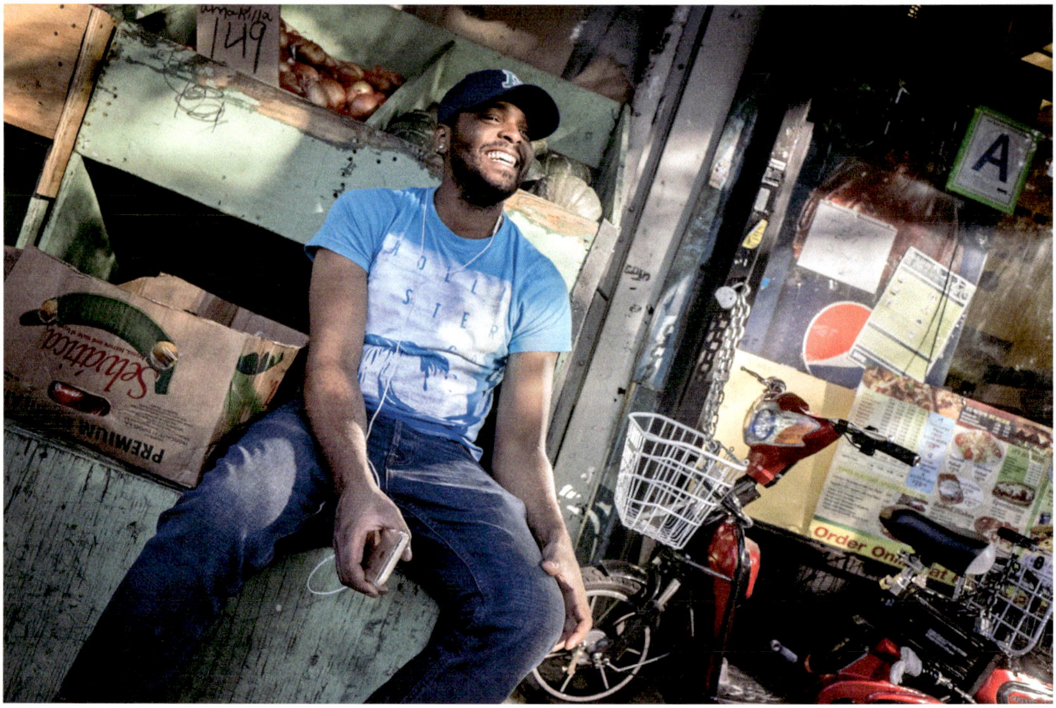

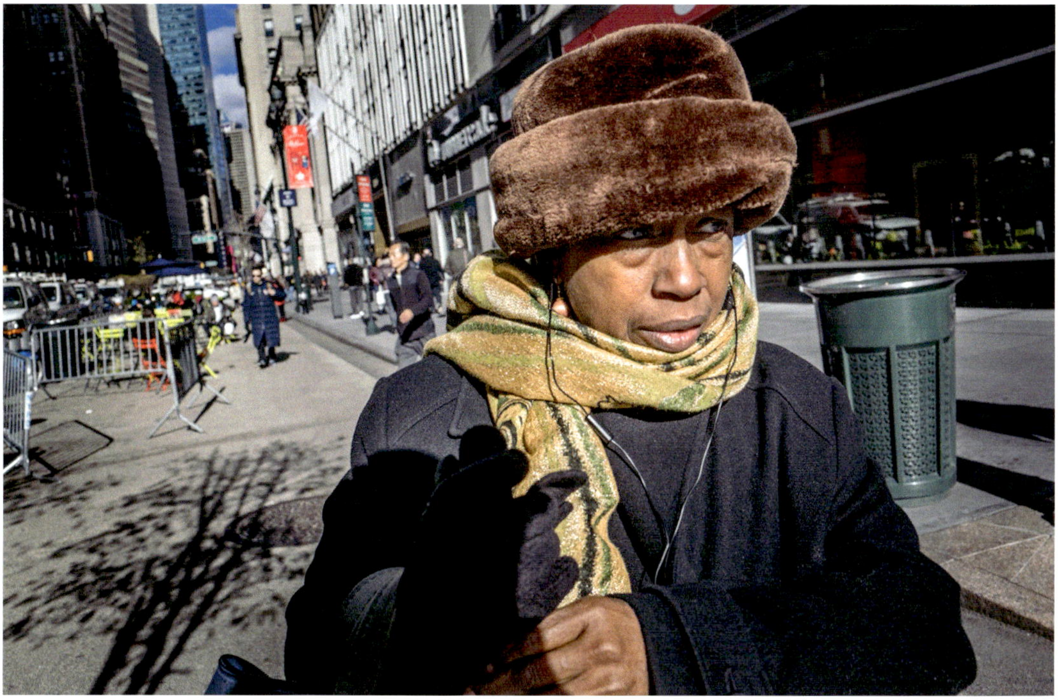

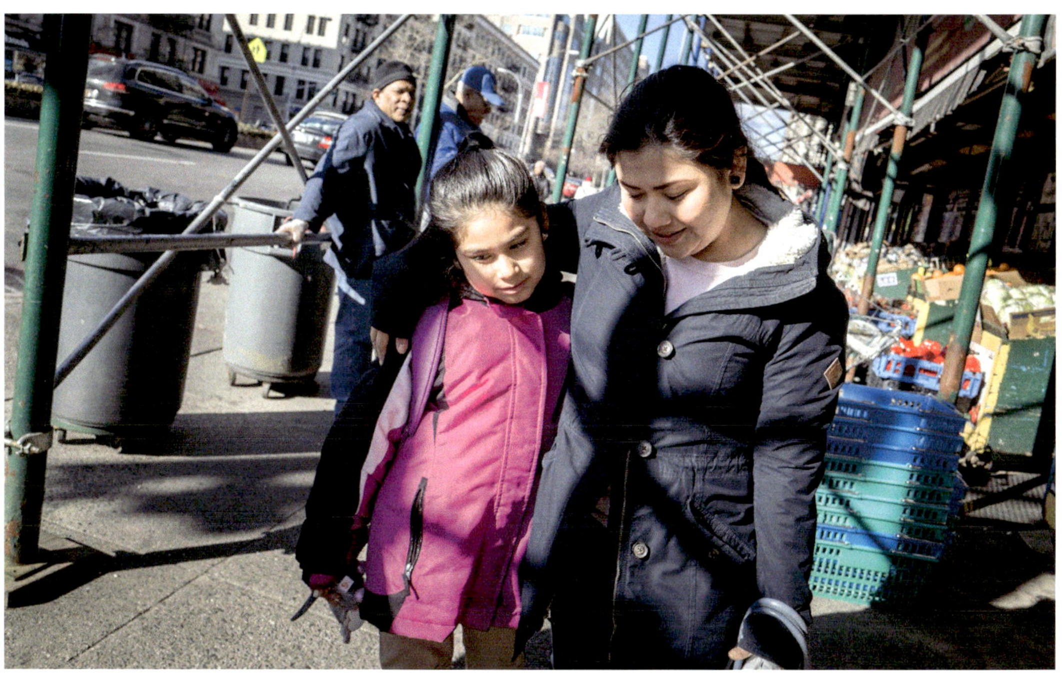

Stylishly bundled against the chill of winter, a woman walks down Broadway.

Two sisters embrace as they walk.

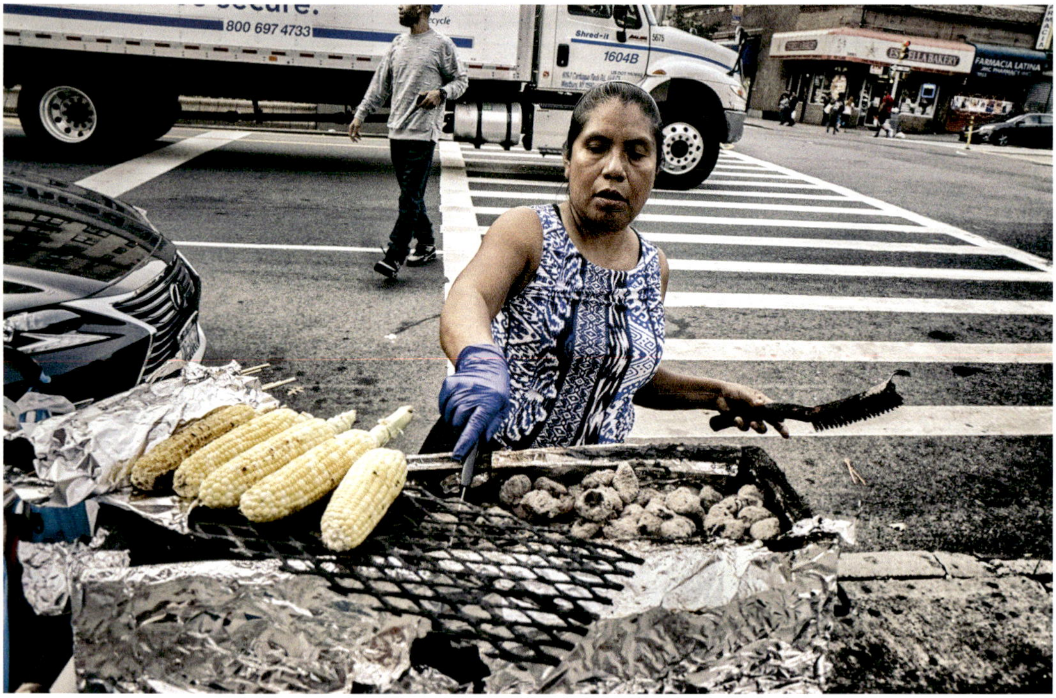

A vendor grills corn along upper Broadway.

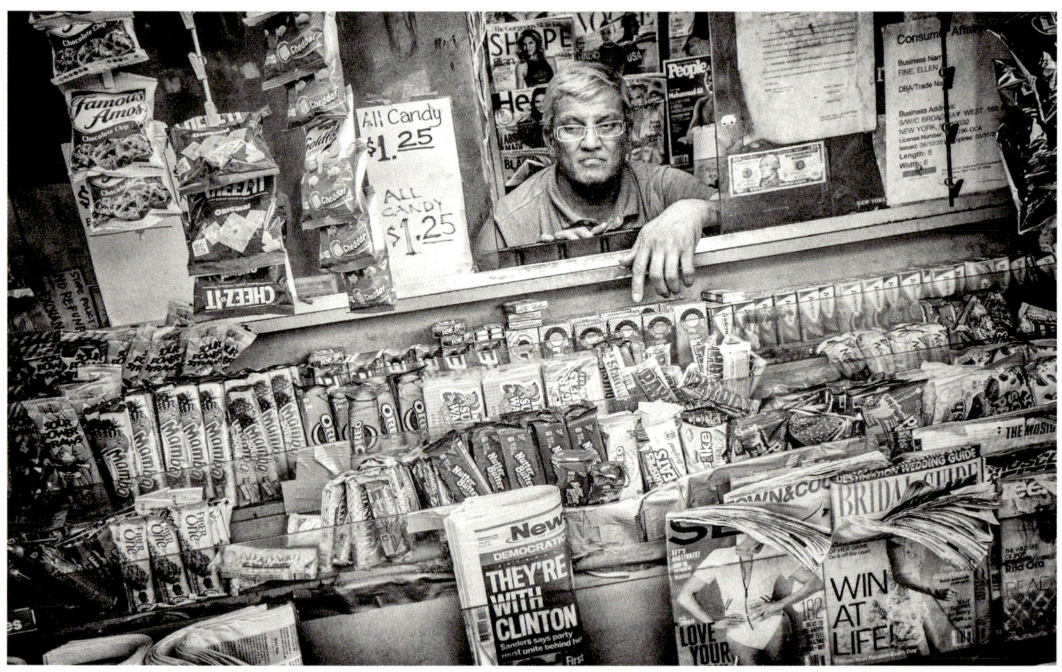

A news vendor in his stall.

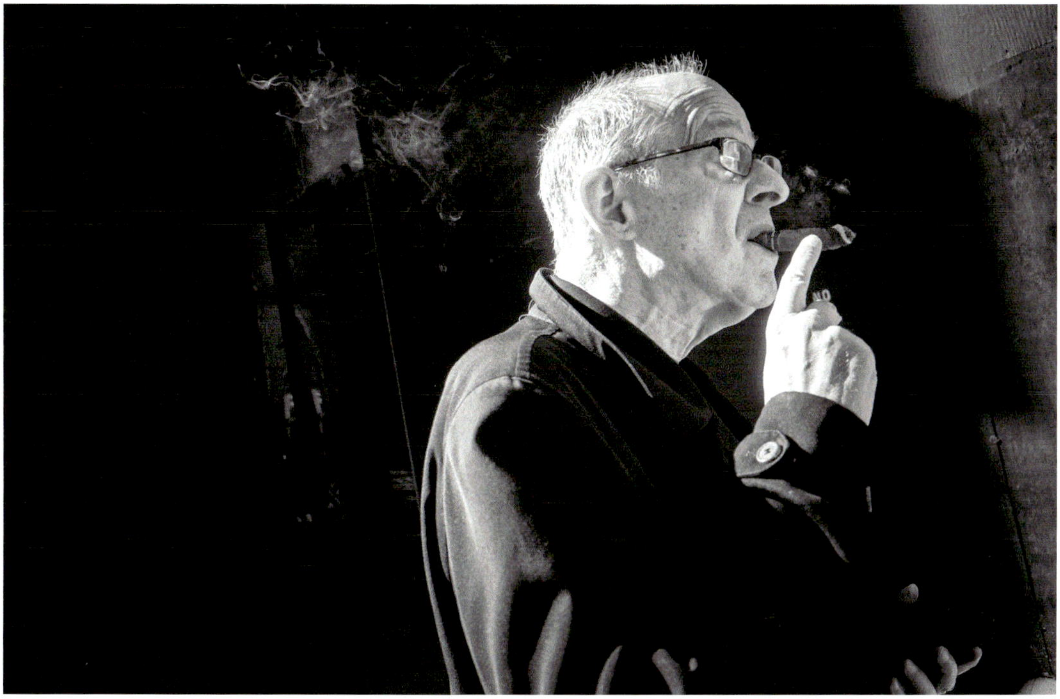

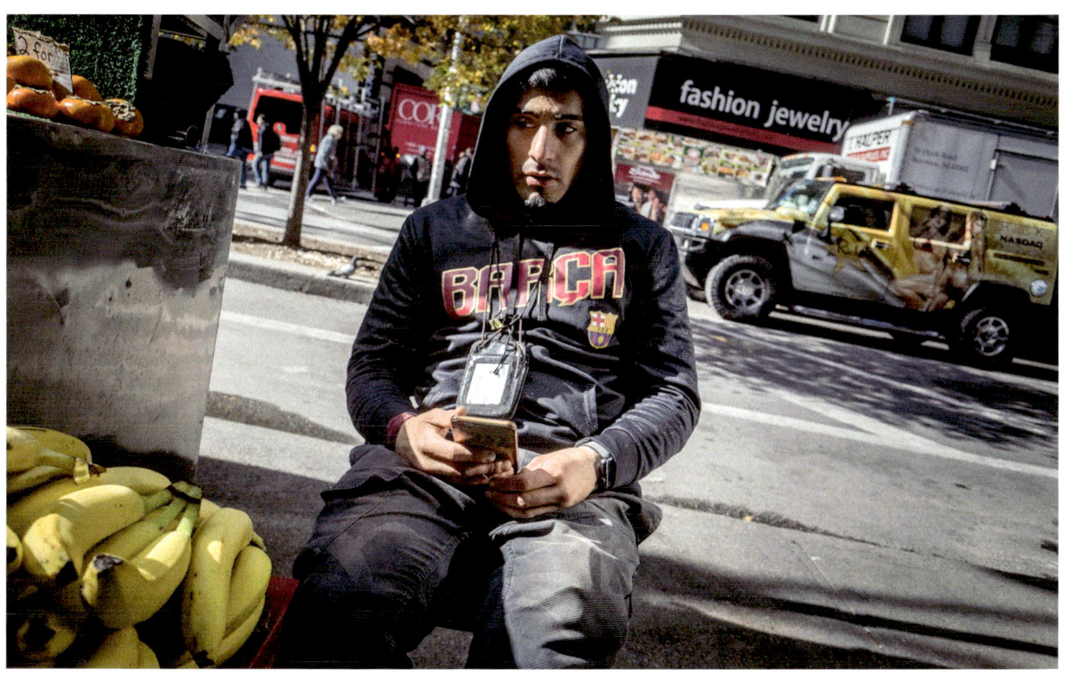

Shadows and smoke frame a man enjoying his cigar.

Vendor selling bananas.

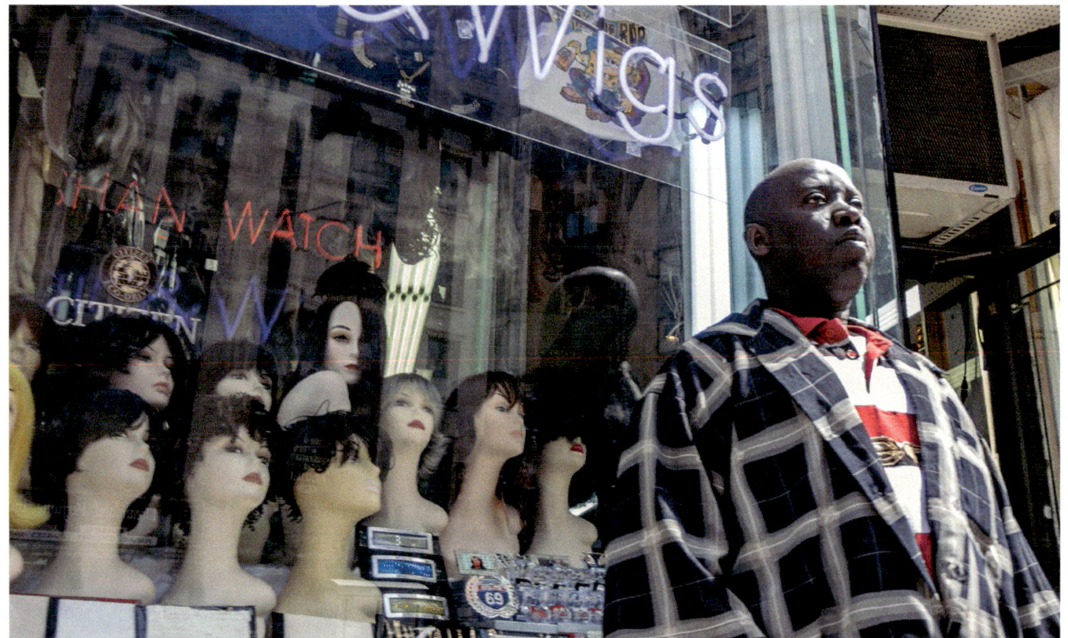

Trying to blend in, a man outside a wig store.

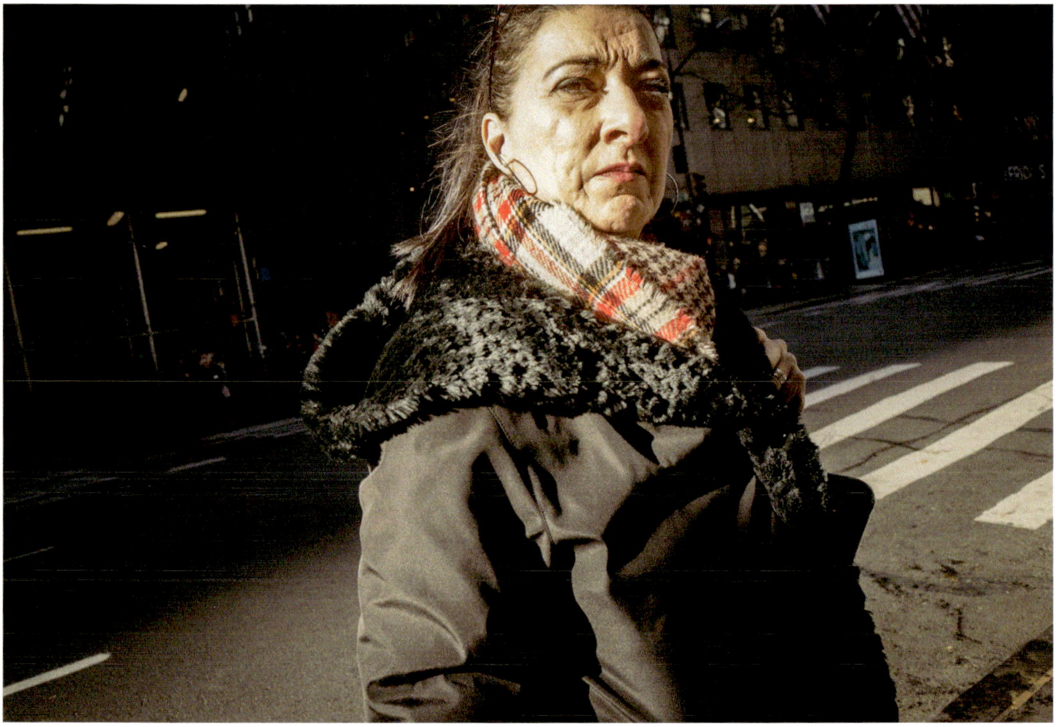

Golden light bathes a woman as she crosses Broadway.

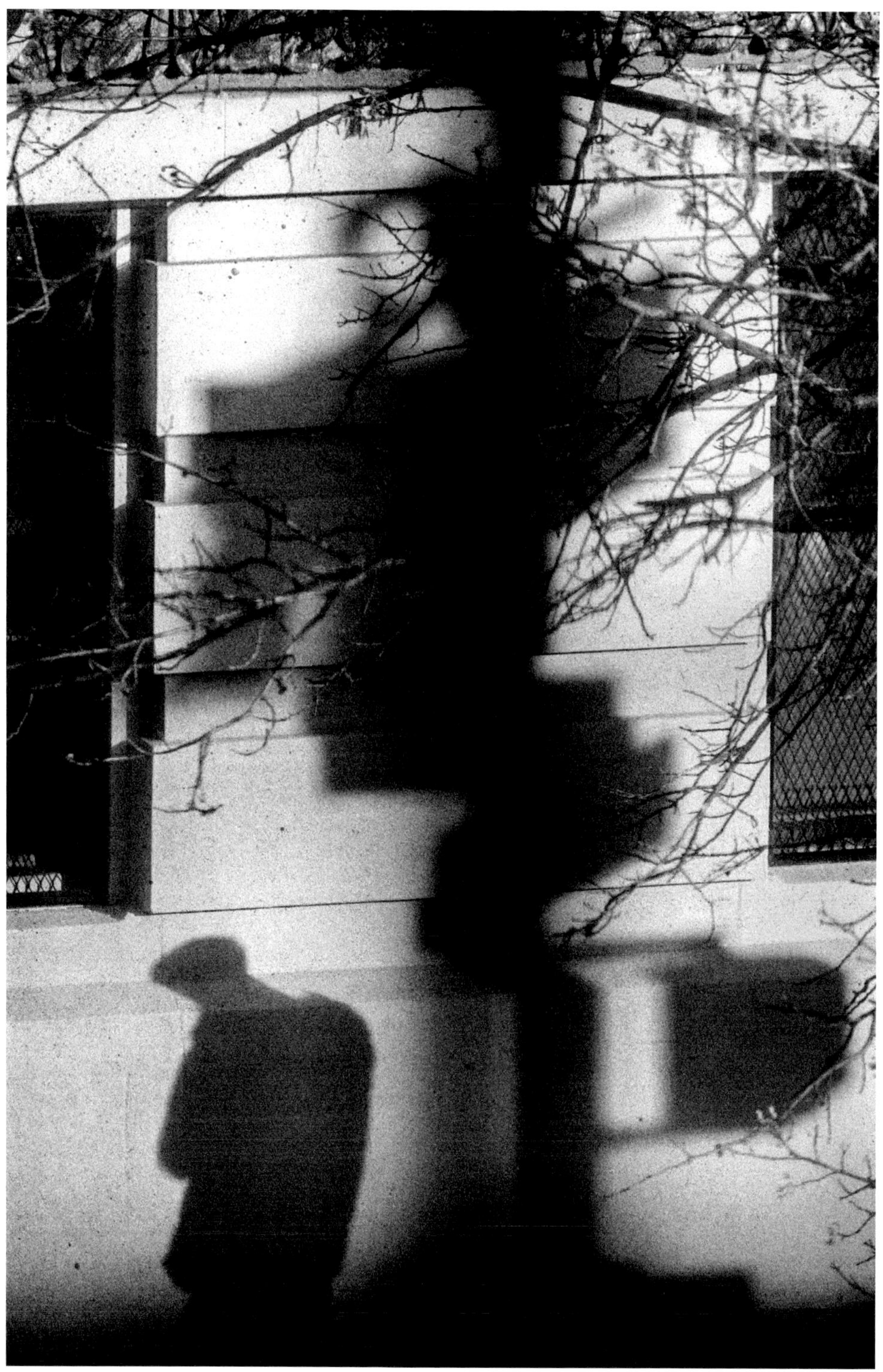

Shadows of a man and streetlamp on a building along Broadway.

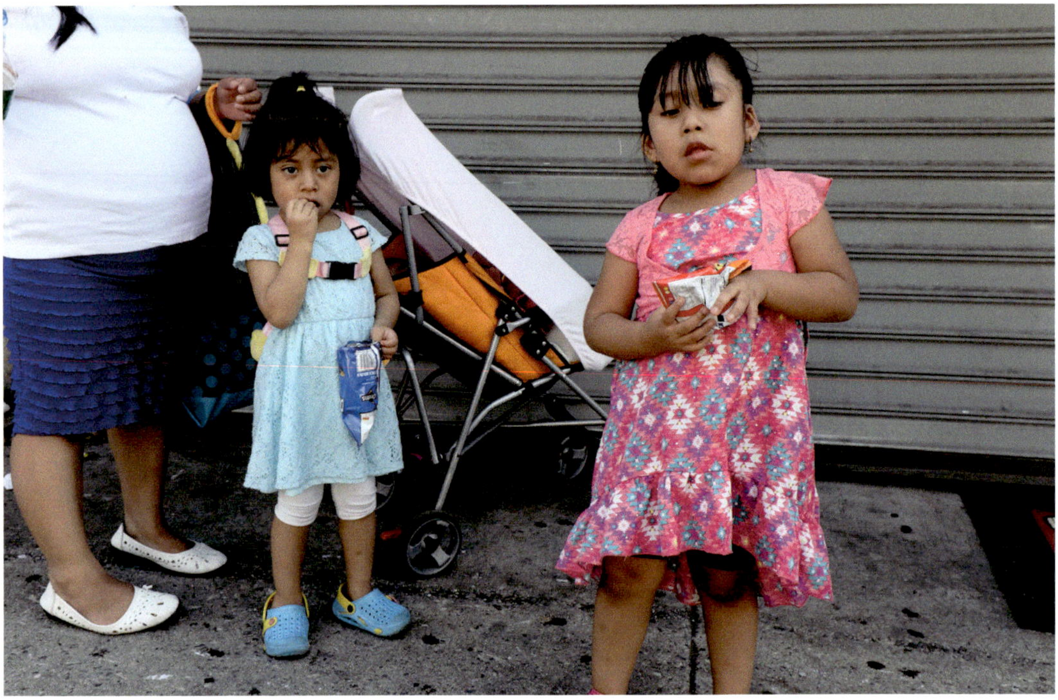

Two girls eat snacks while they and their mother wait for a bus.

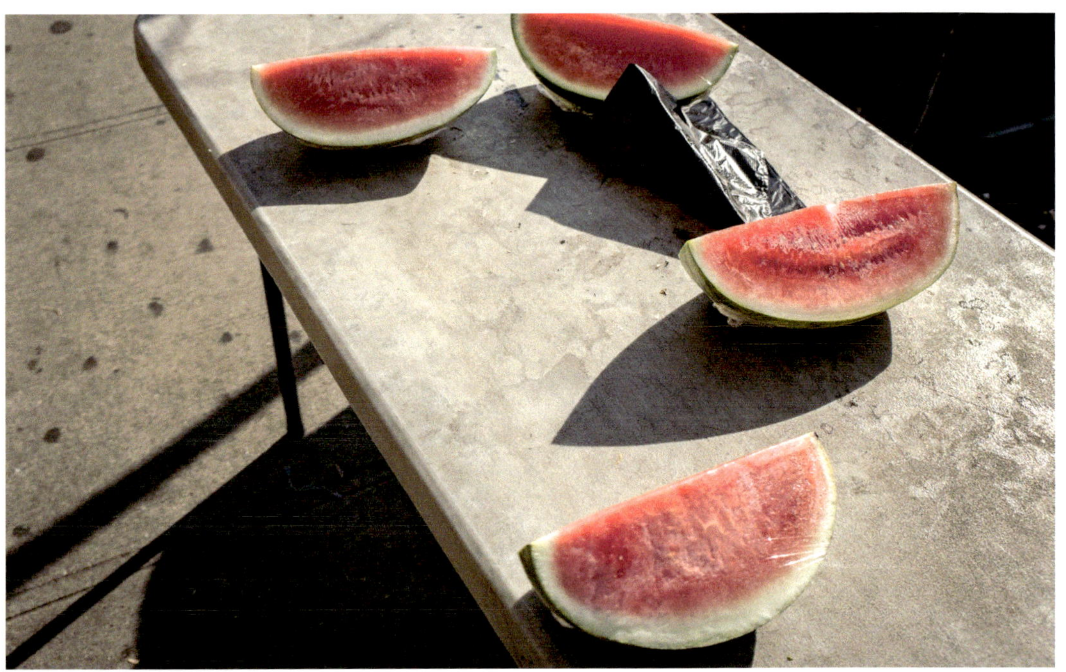

Watermelon quarters are displayed on a table for sale.

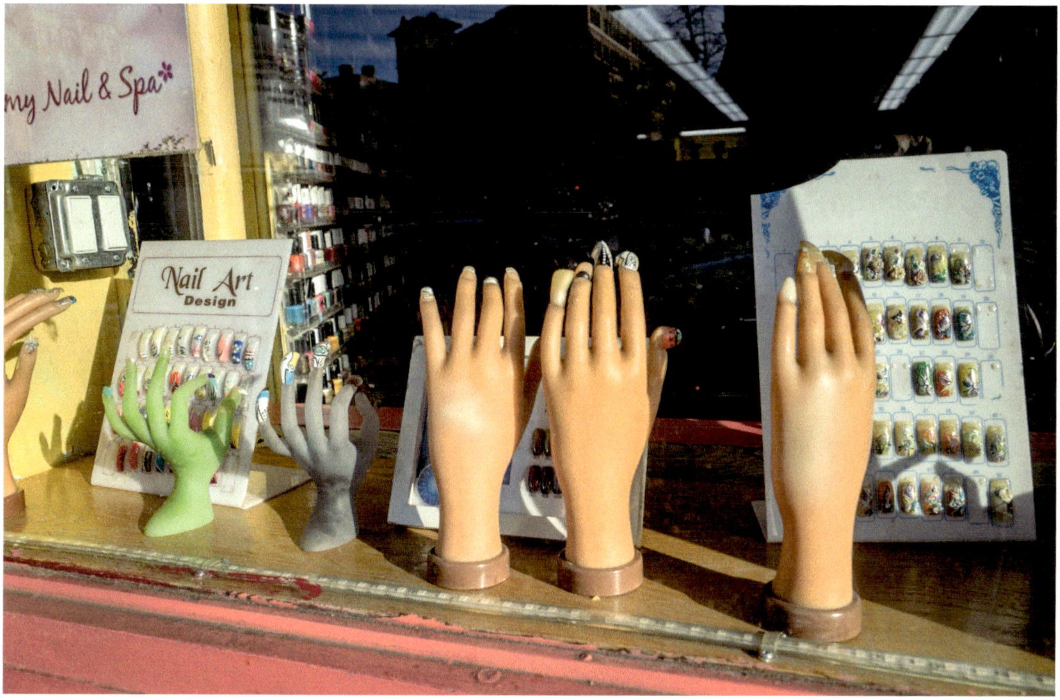

Window display of nail tips in a nail salon.

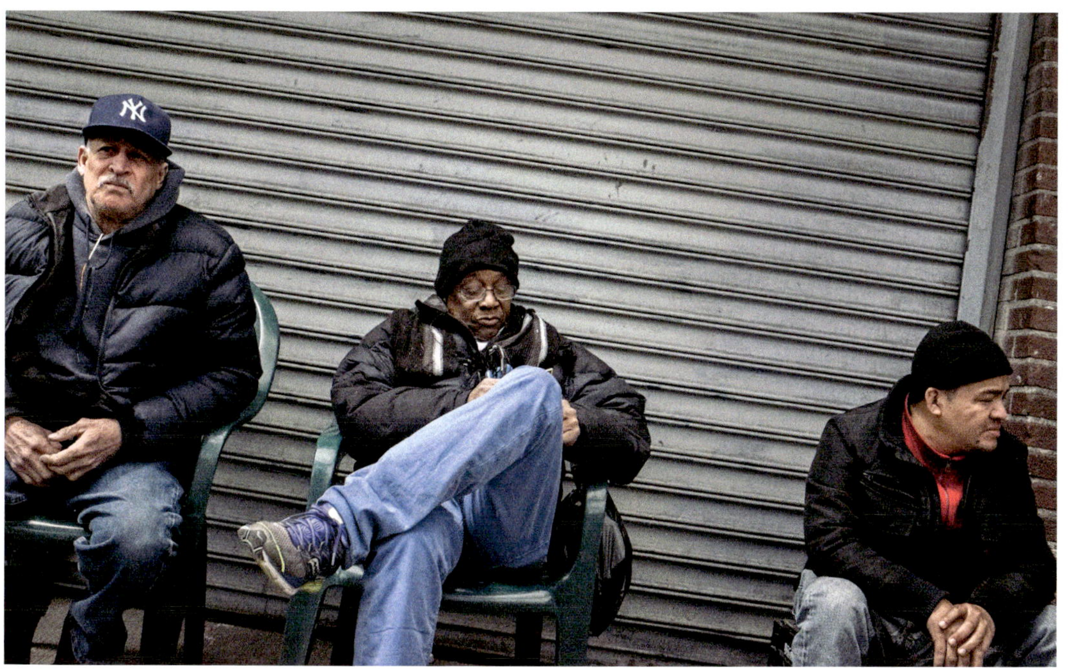

Three men pass the time watching the world go by.

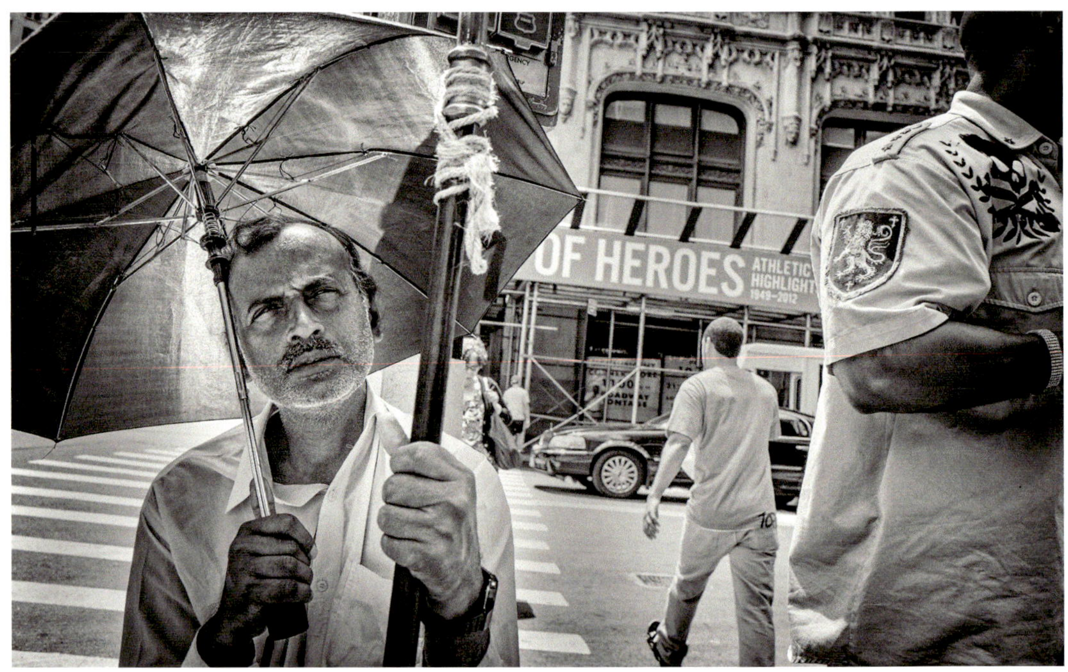

A man shields himself form the sun holding an umbrella and the pole of a placard advertisement.

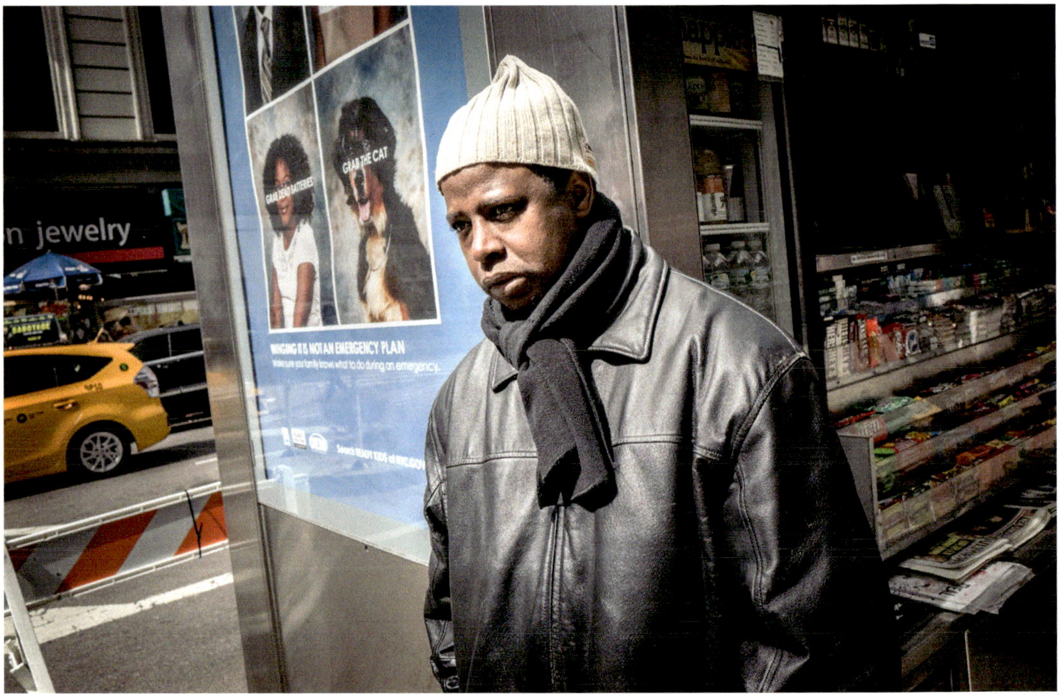

Newsstand vendor standing in the sun outside his stall.

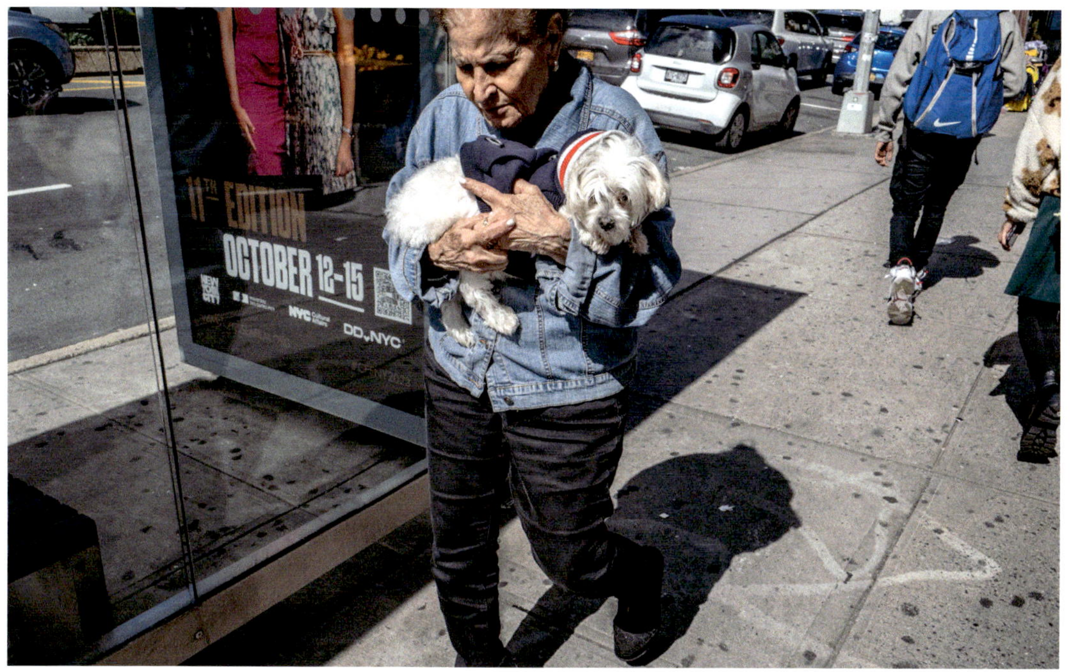

A woman cradles her dog walking along Broadway.

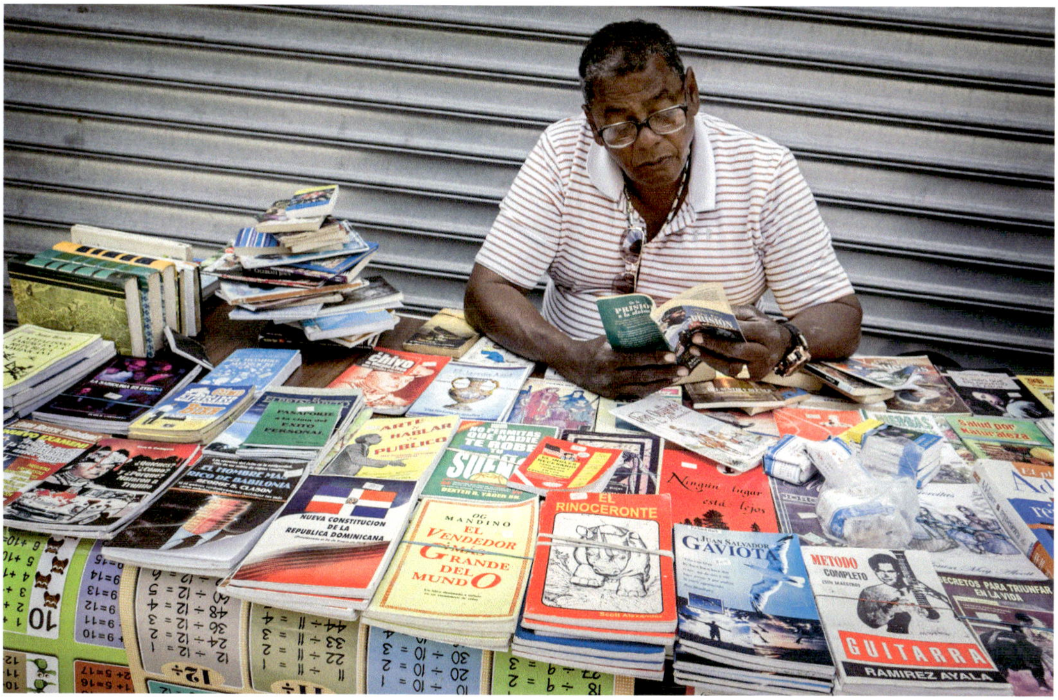

Looking through a book, a street bookseller displays his wares.

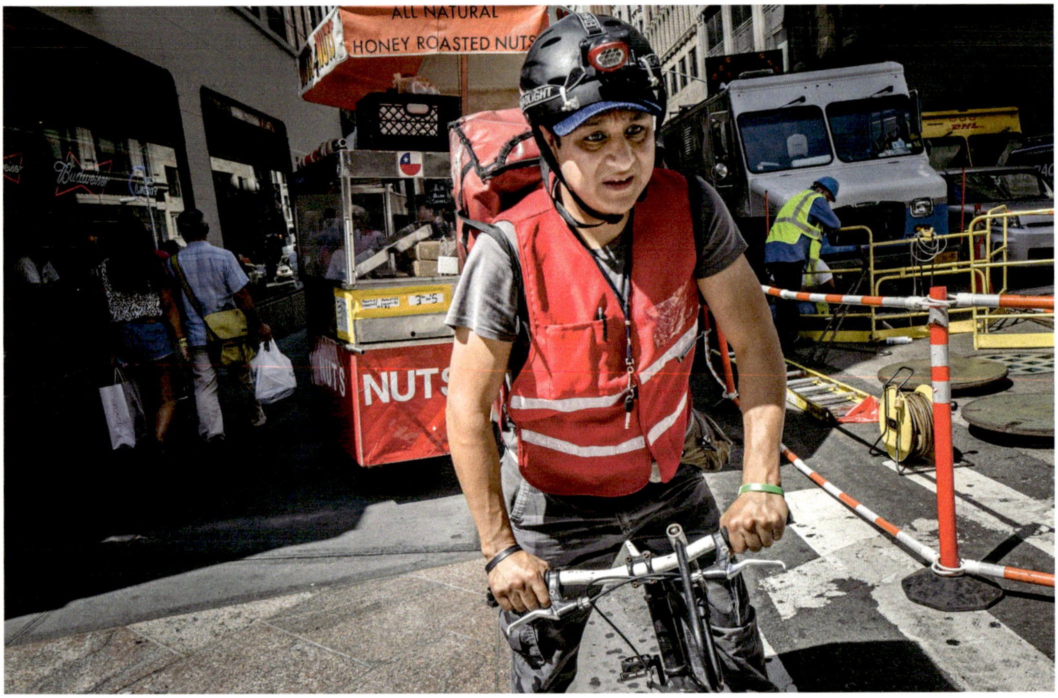

Navigating the streets, a food deliveryman waits at a red light.

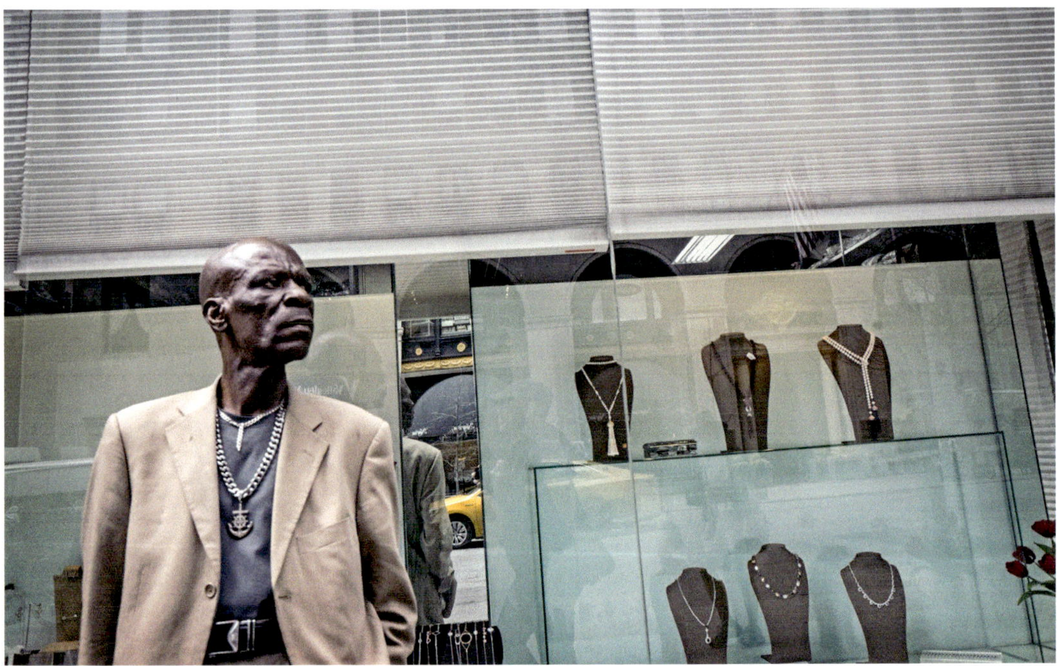

Outside a jewelry store.

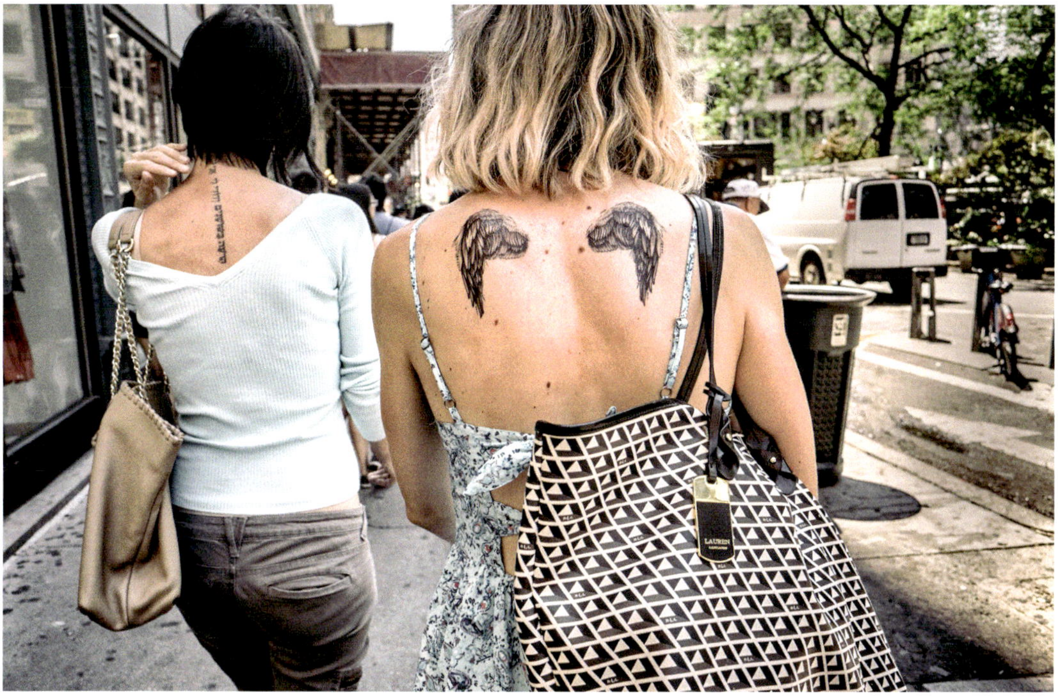

Women with back tattoos.

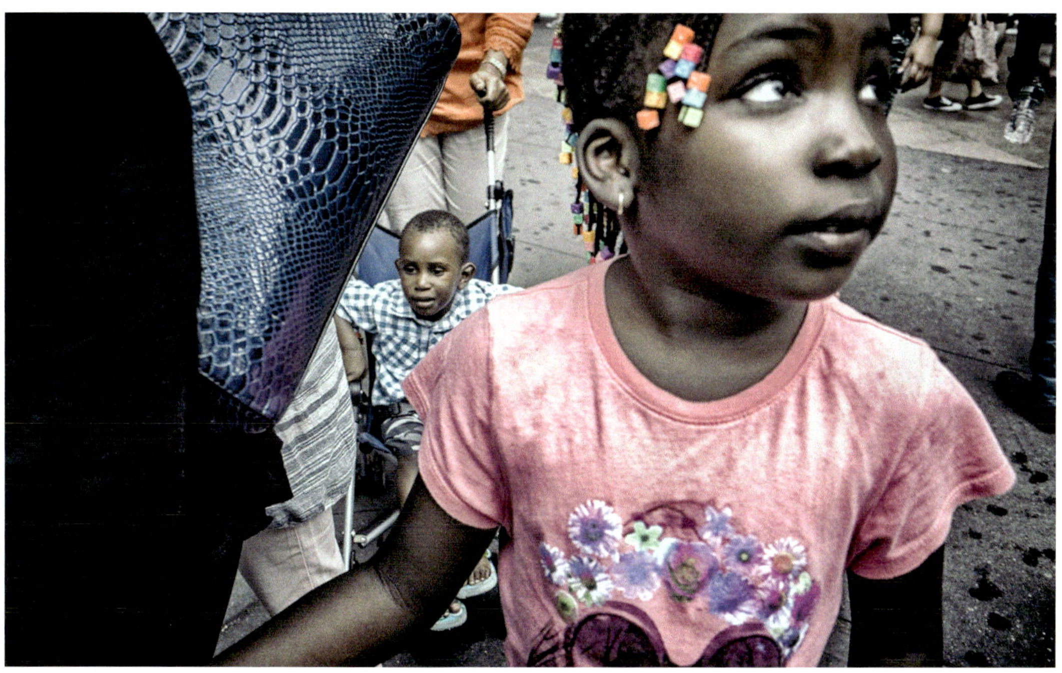

Children walk with their parents.

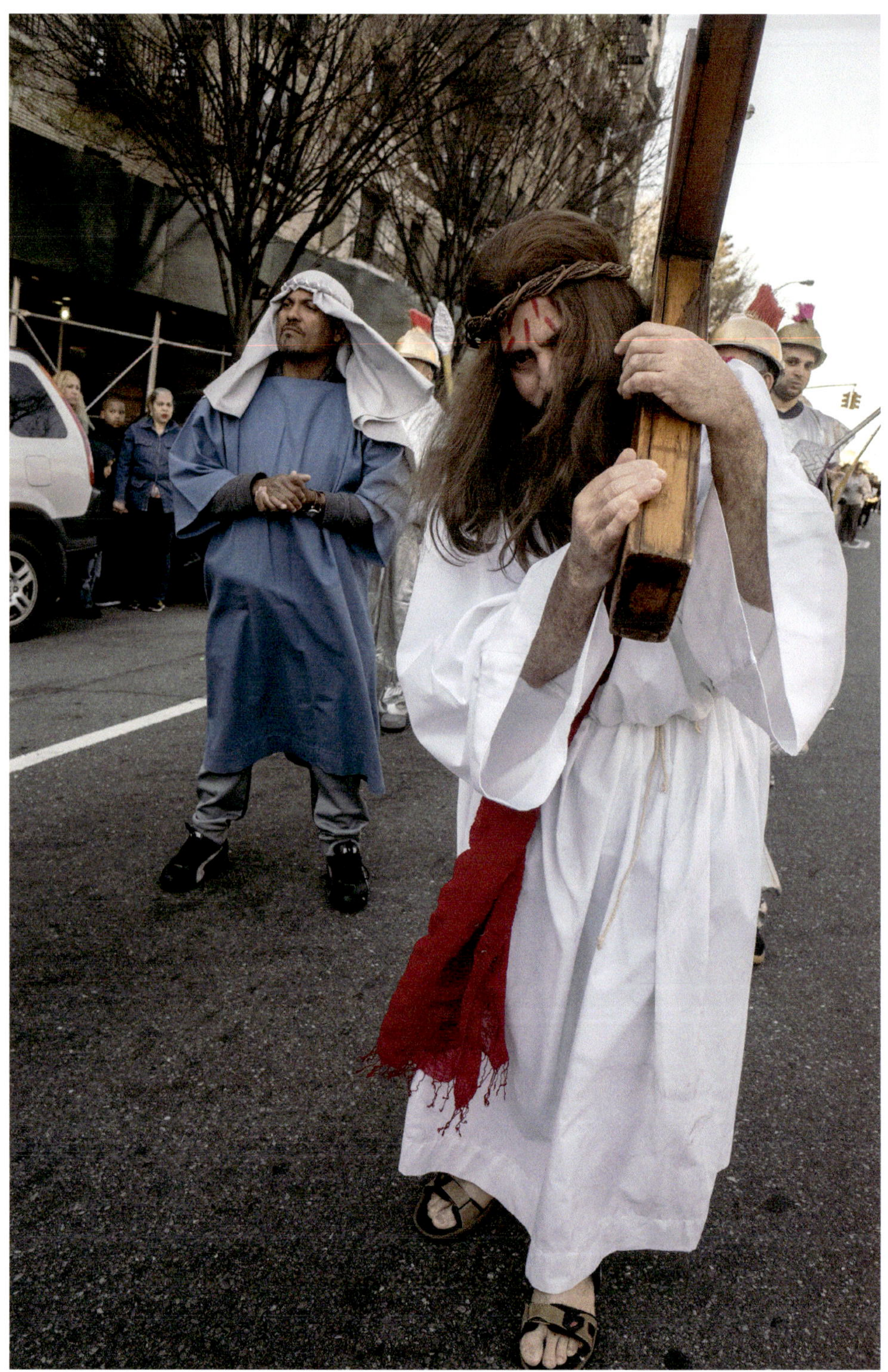

An Easter procession makes its way down Broadway.

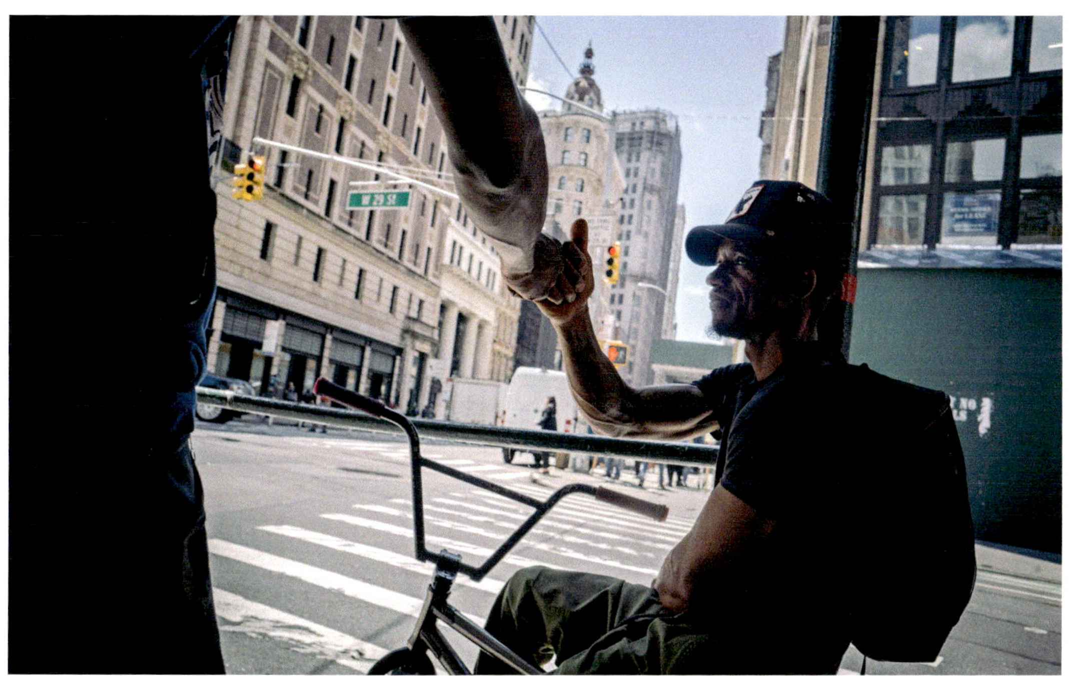

Two men give a fist bump greeting.

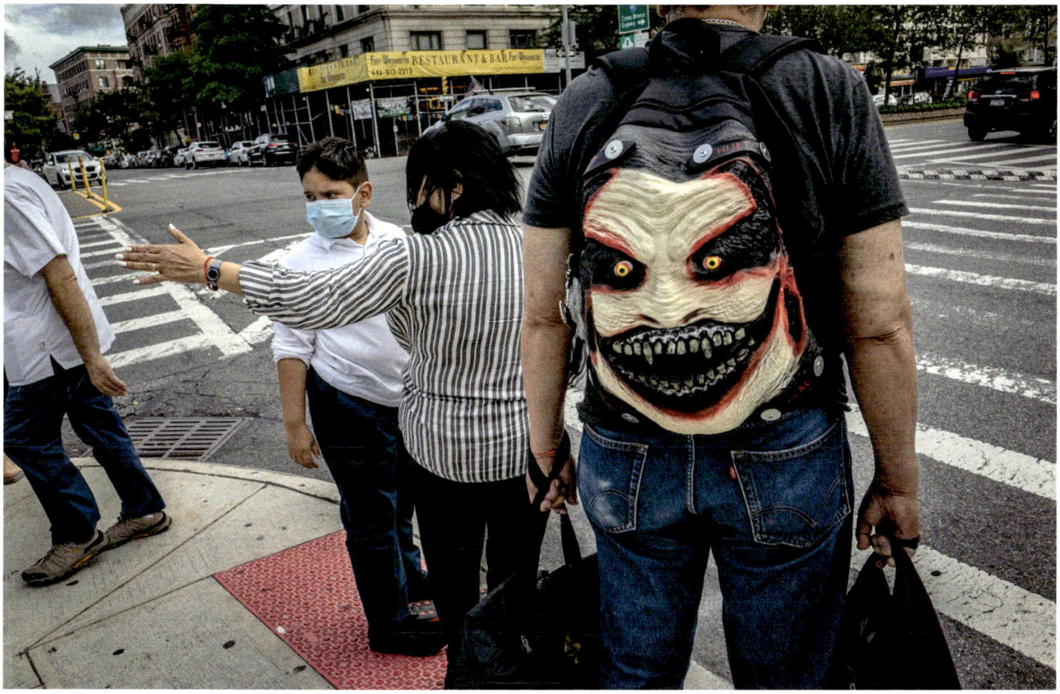

A man wears "The Fiend" backpack.

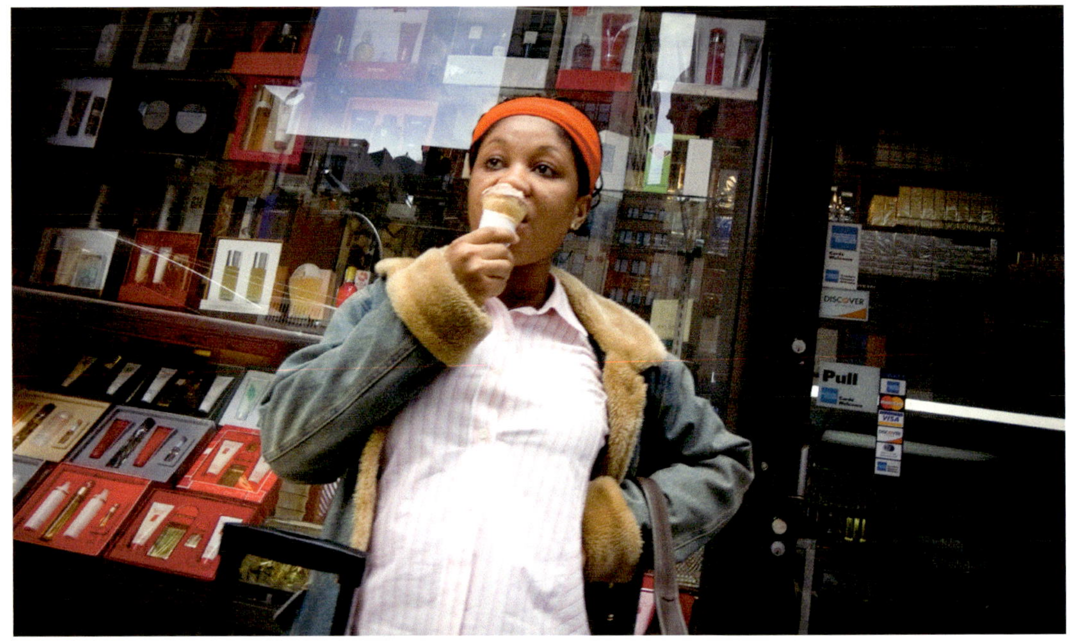

A woman eats an ice cream cone in front of a perfume shop.

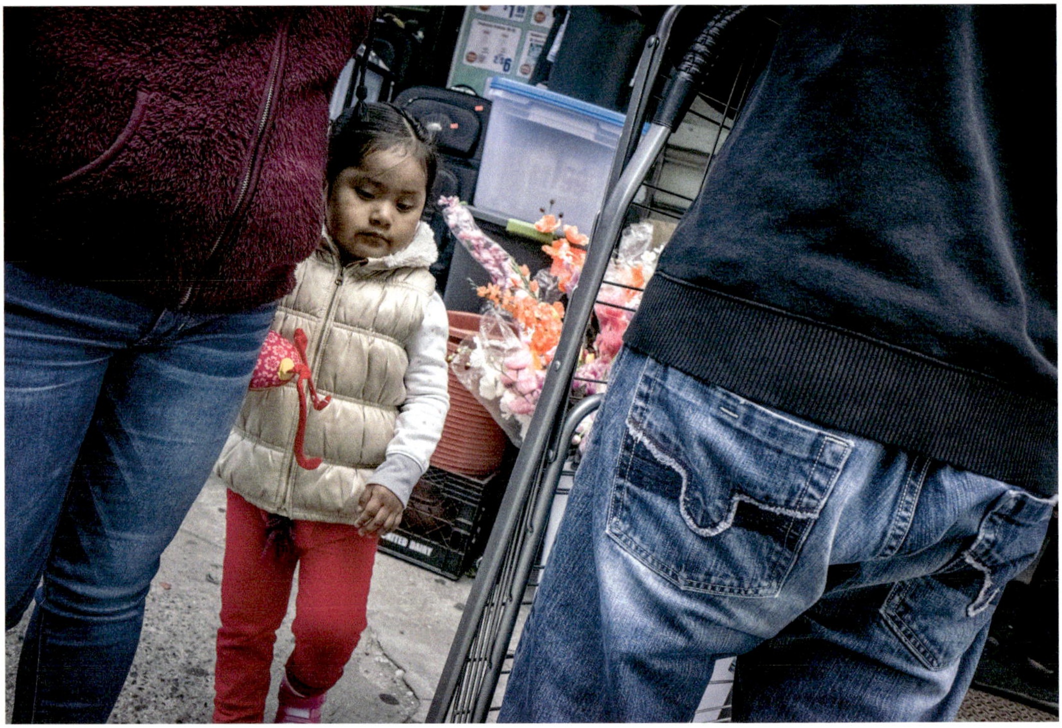

A child strolls with her mother on Mother's Day.

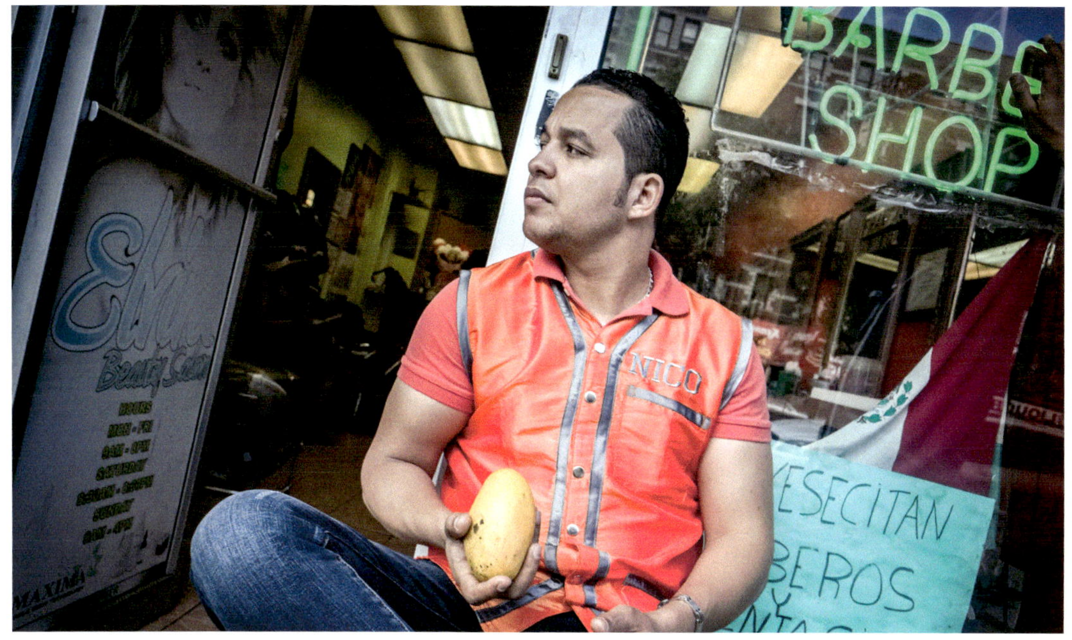

Tossing a mango in his hands, a barber waits for customers.

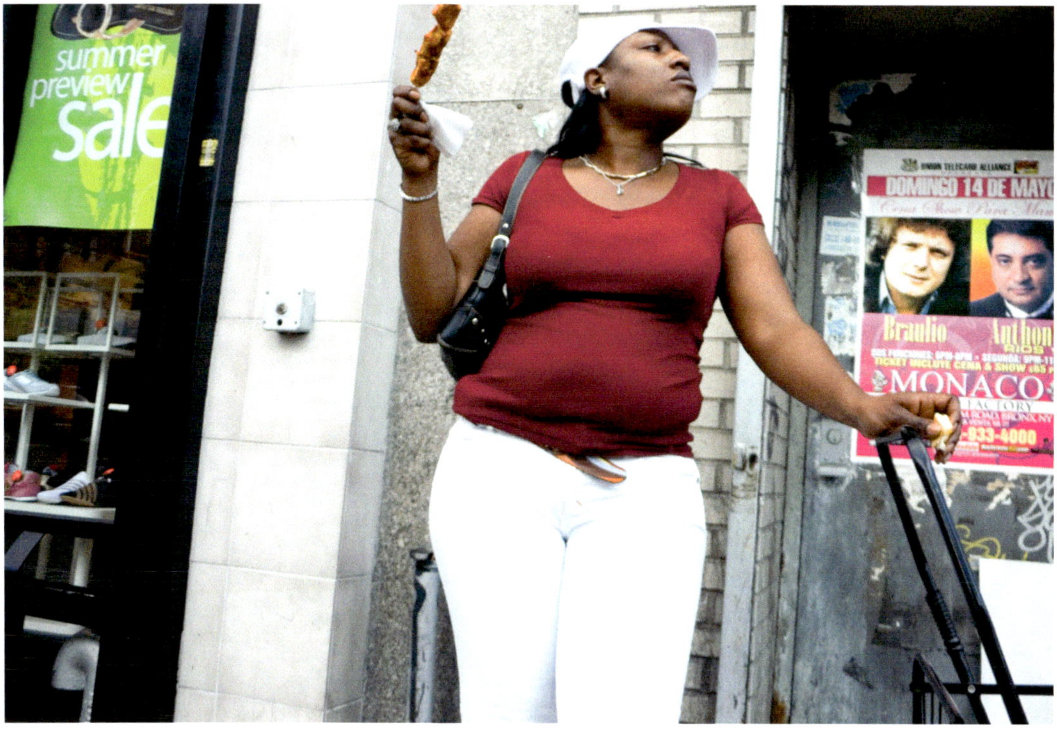

Standing proud, a woman holds grilled chicken on a skewer.

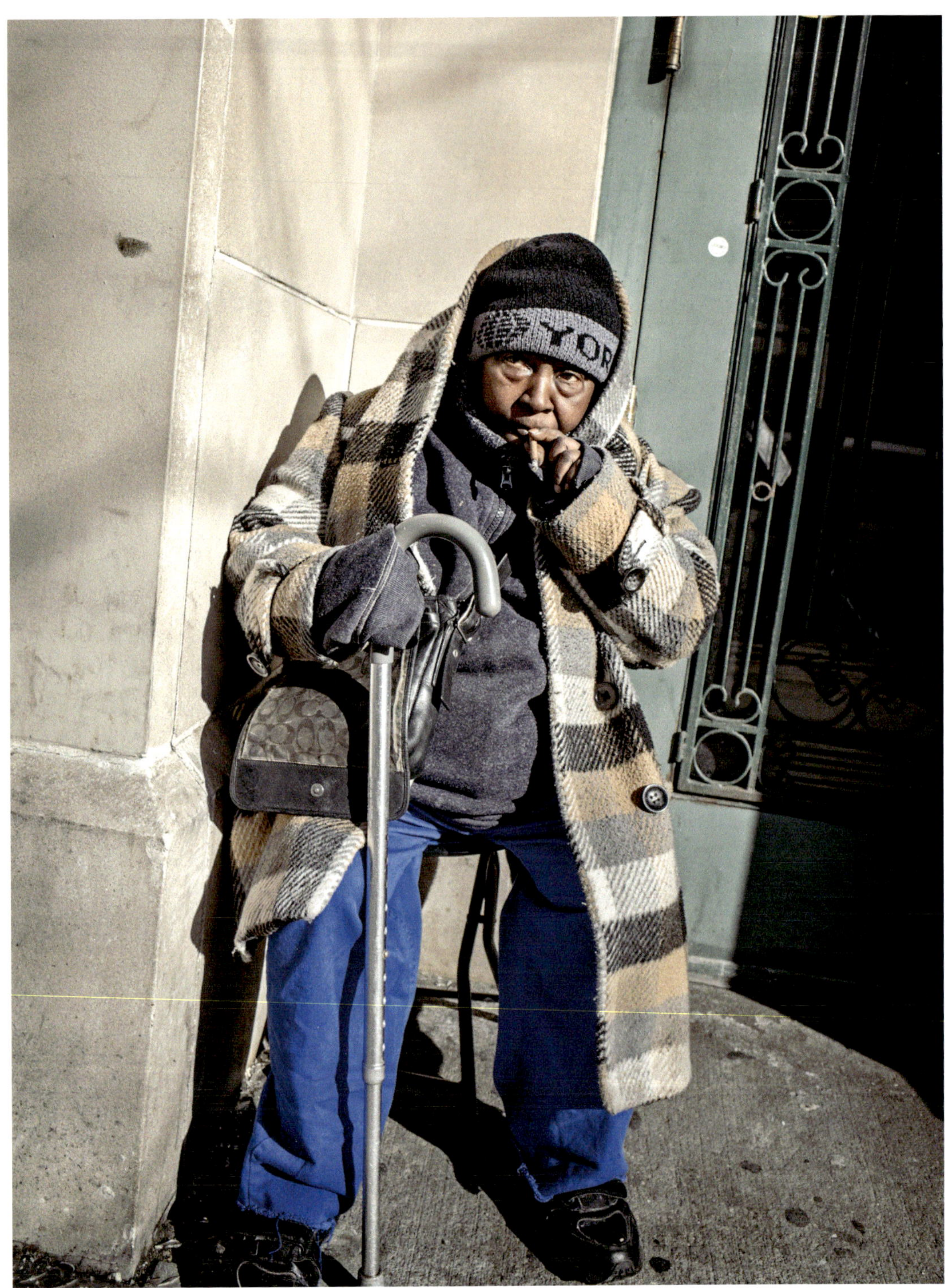

A woman smokes a cigar in the shelter of her apartment building entrance.

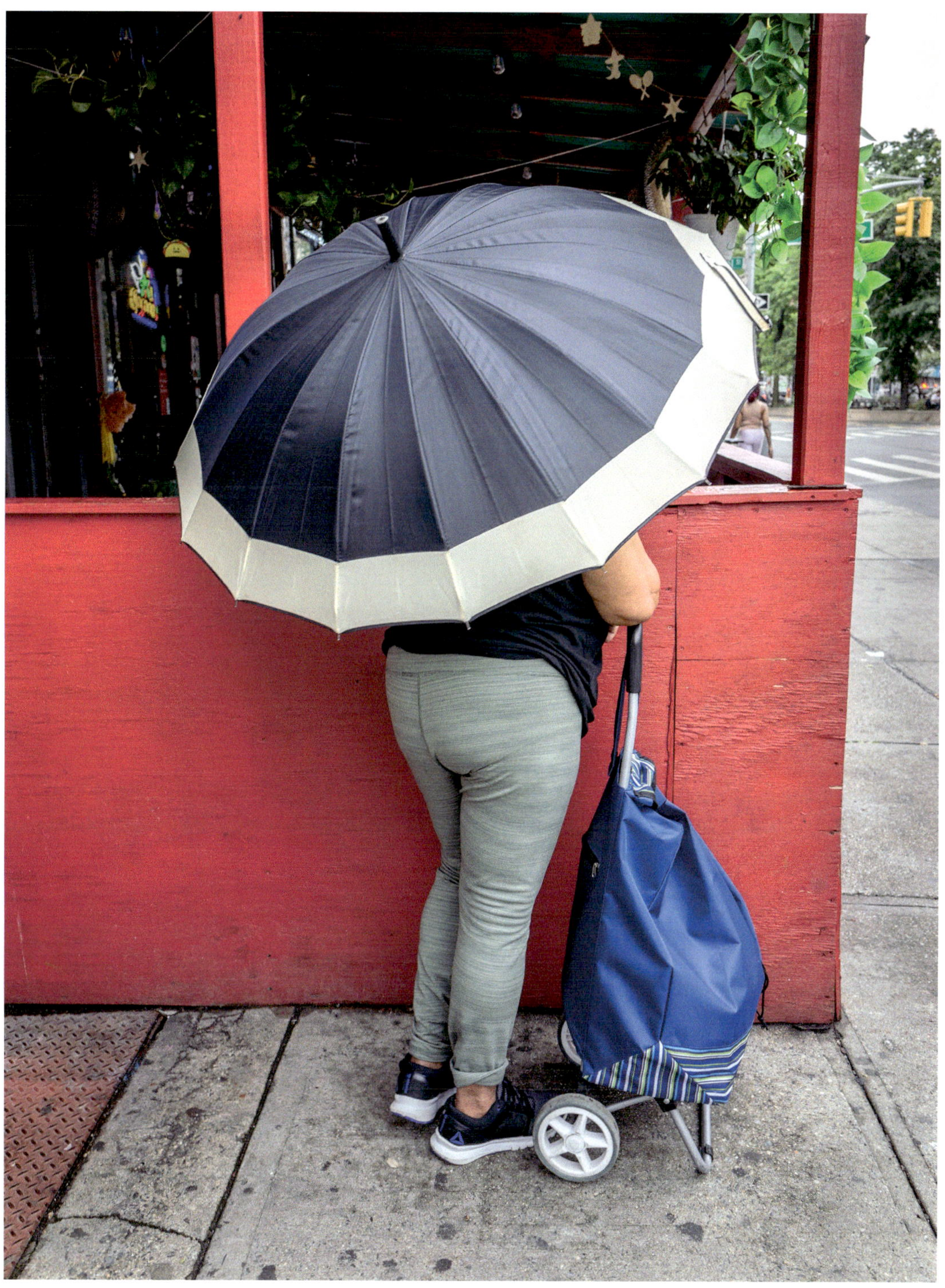

When I saw this woman shielding herself from the rain under her umbrella, her stance reminded me of Manuel Alvarez Bravo's image of *The Daughter of the Dancers*.

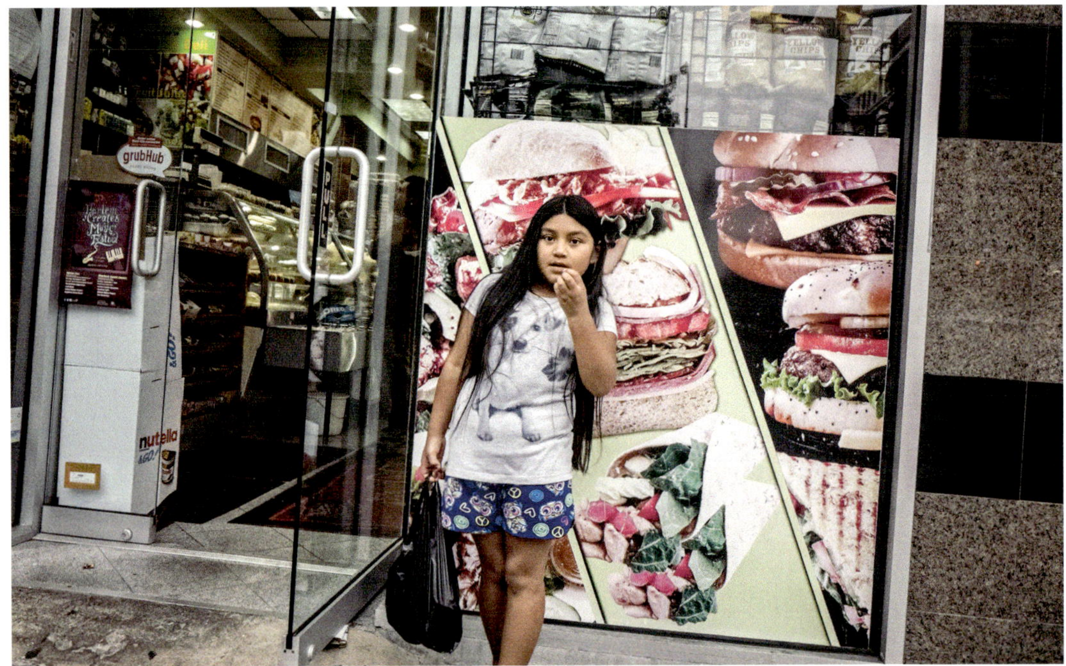

A girl waits for friends in front of a deli.

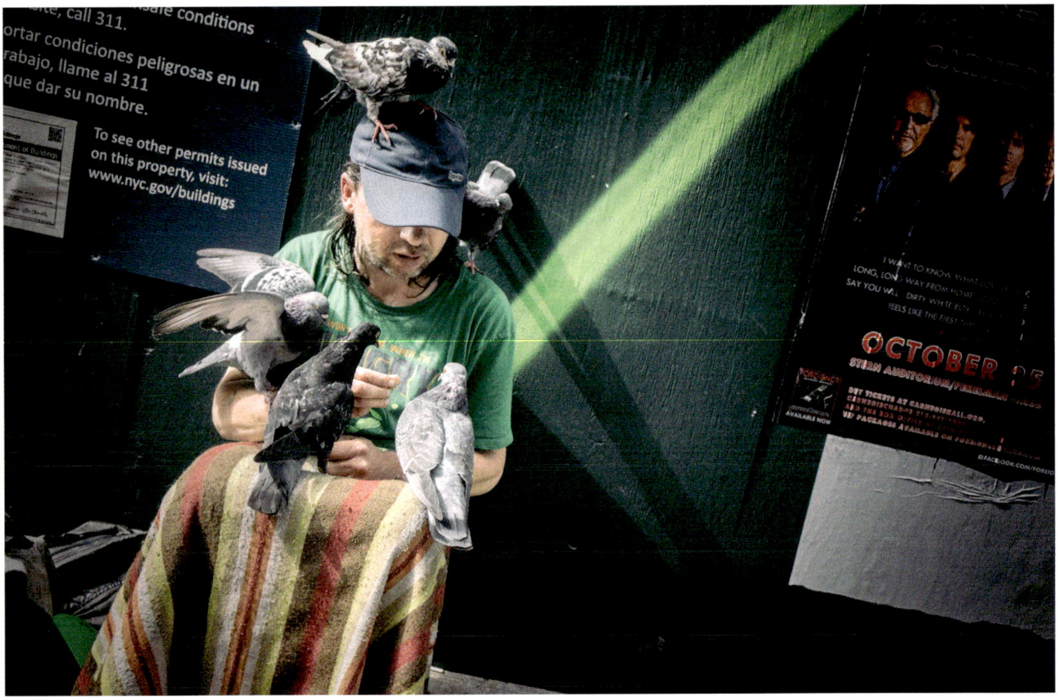

A man sits on a city sidewalk, pigeons perched on his arms, shoulders, and his hat.

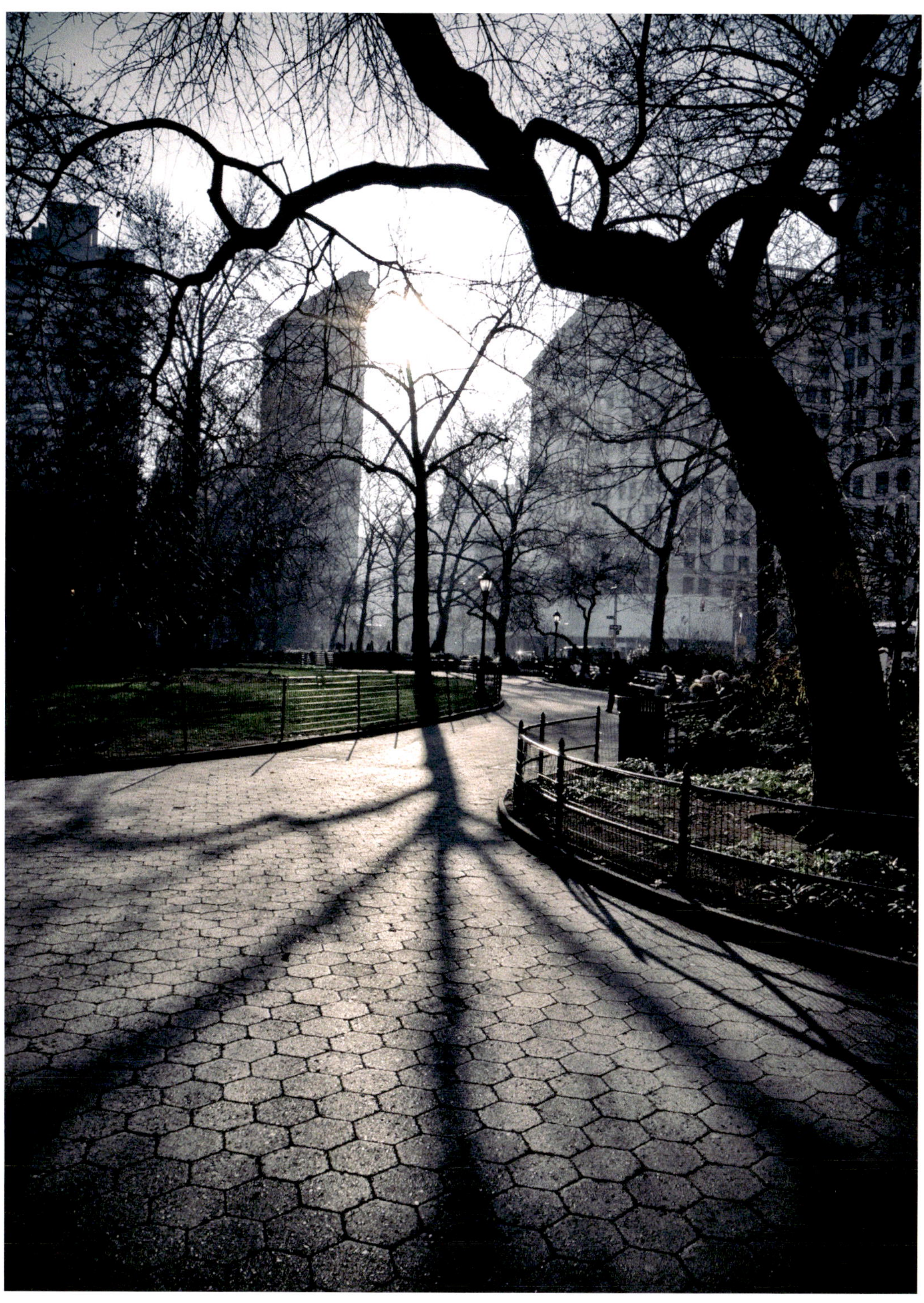

The Flatiron Building as seen from Madison Square Park.

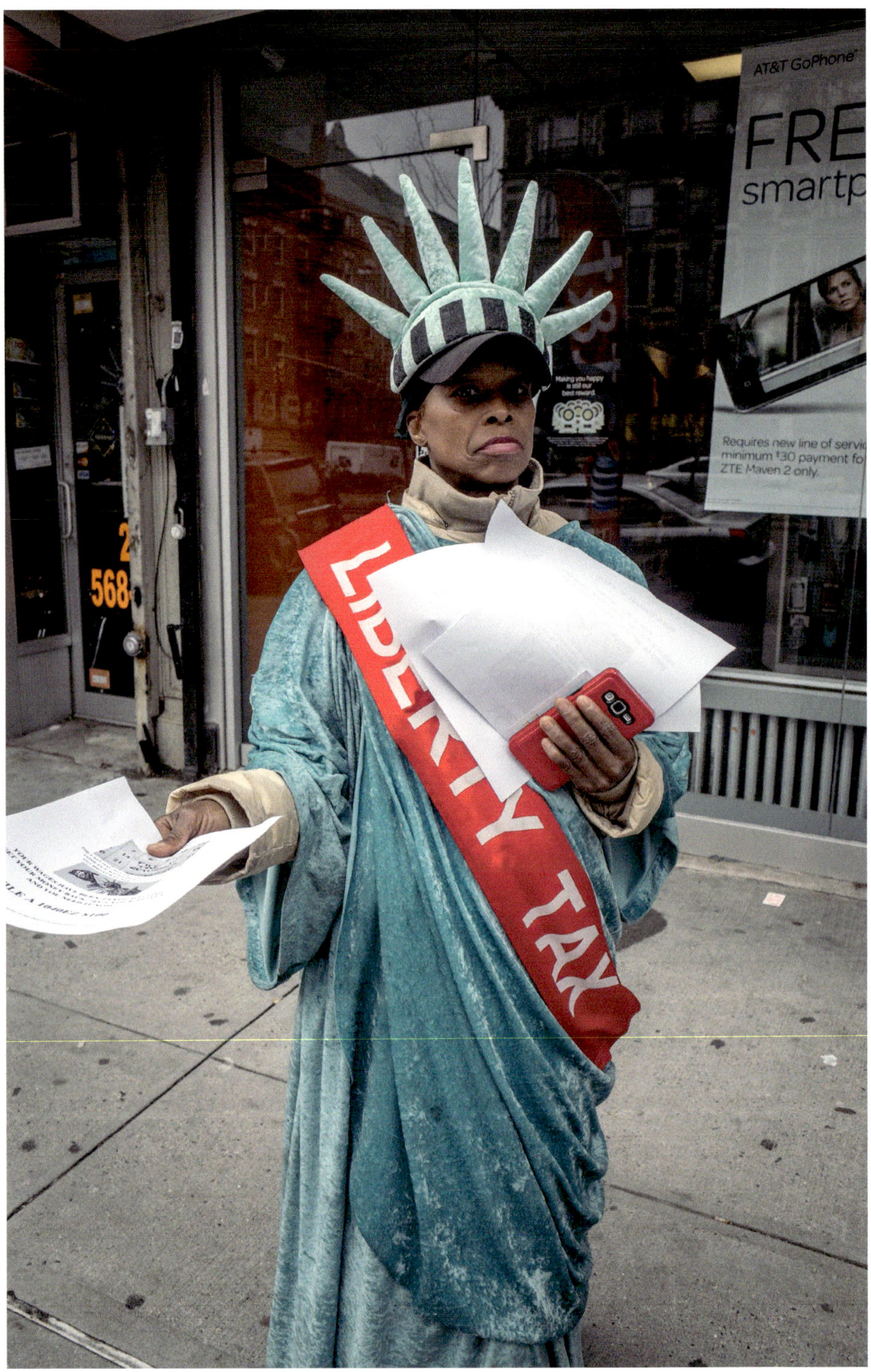

A woman dressed as the Statue of Liberty advertising a tax service.

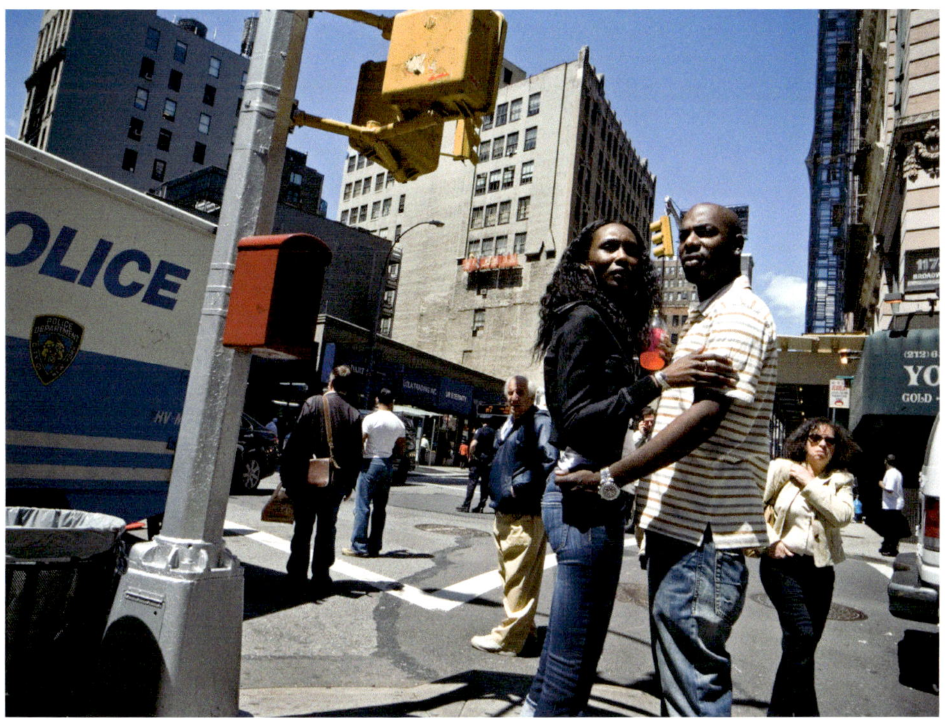

A couple embraces on a bustling New York City street, their gaze meeting the camera with an air of quiet confidence.

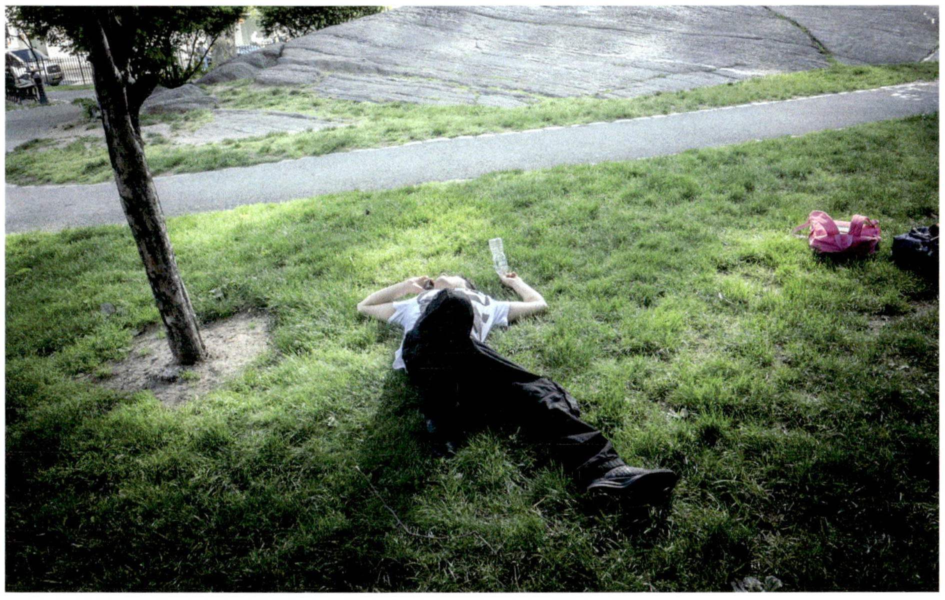

Green spaces are rare in NYC. Here a man lies on the grass of Mitchel Square.

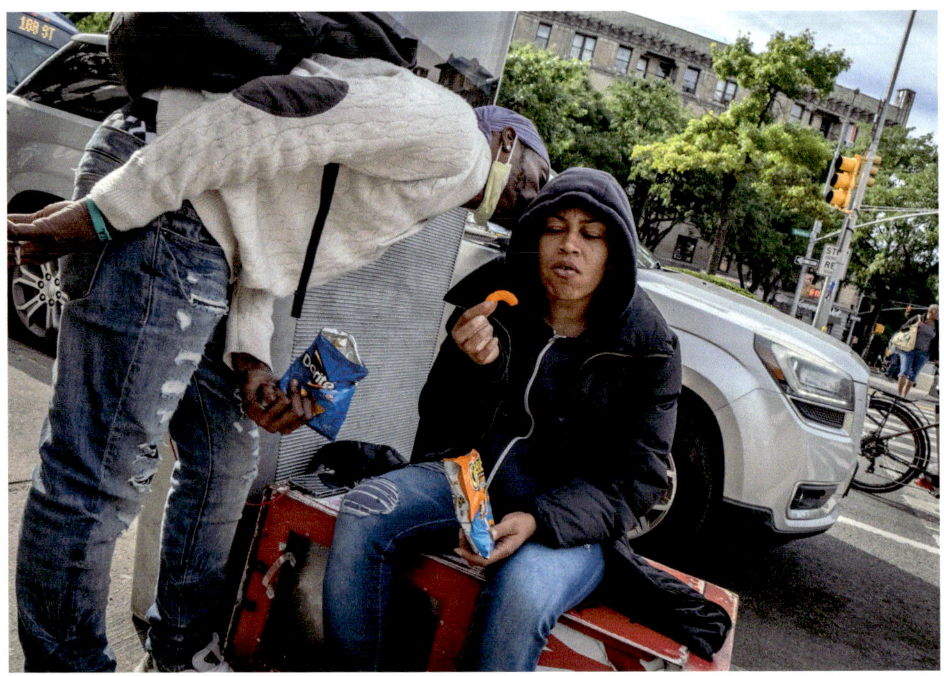

Two friends share a snack while charging their phone at a street kiosk.

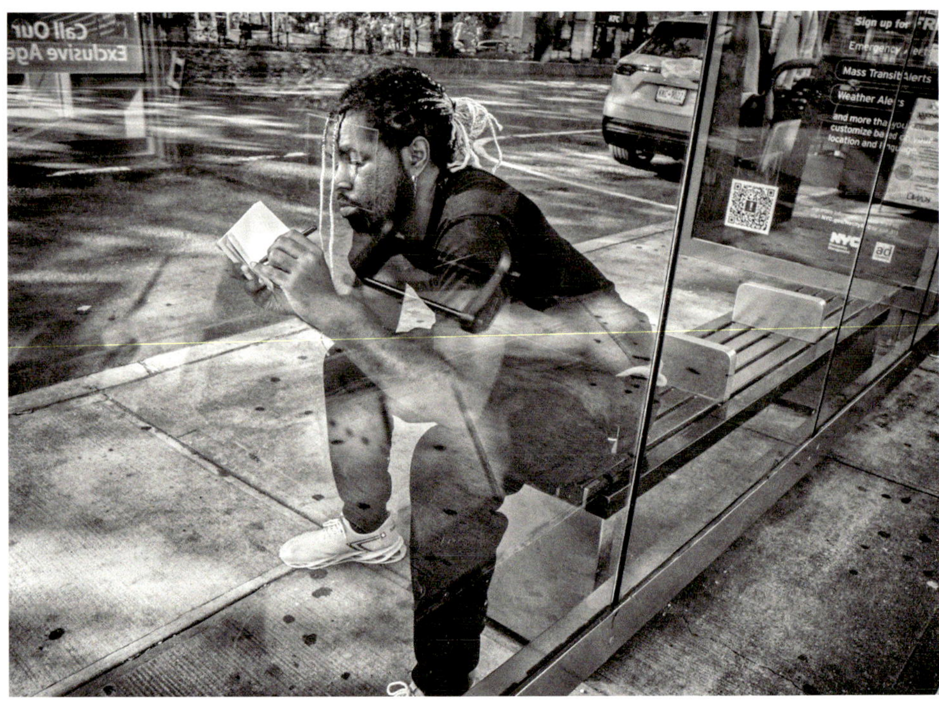

Sitting in a bus kiosk, a man scribbles notes in a small book.

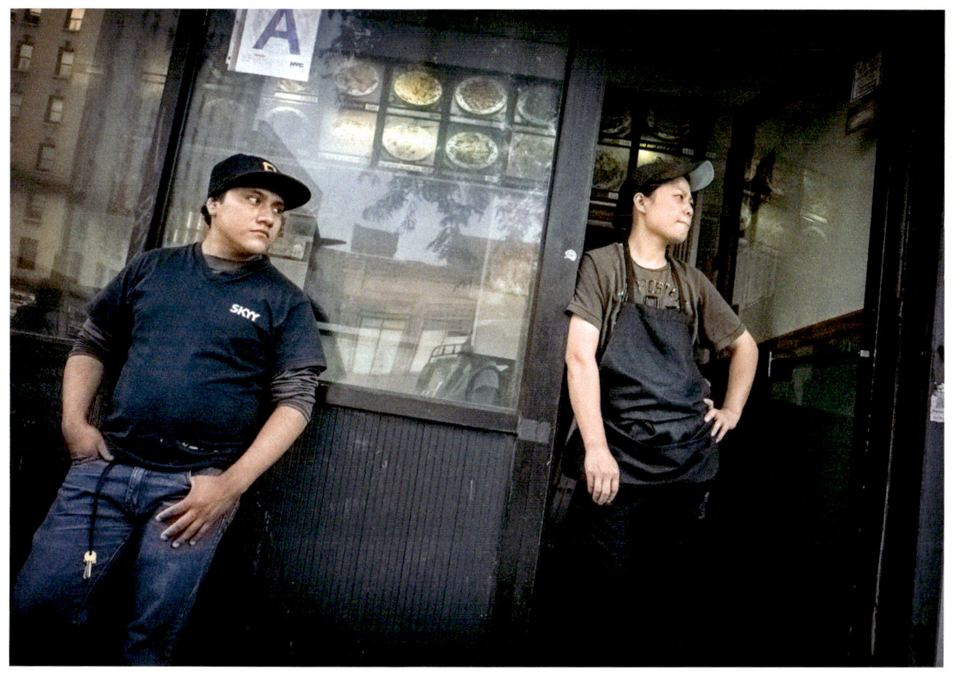

A chef and a deliveryman wait for business outside a Chinese restaurant.

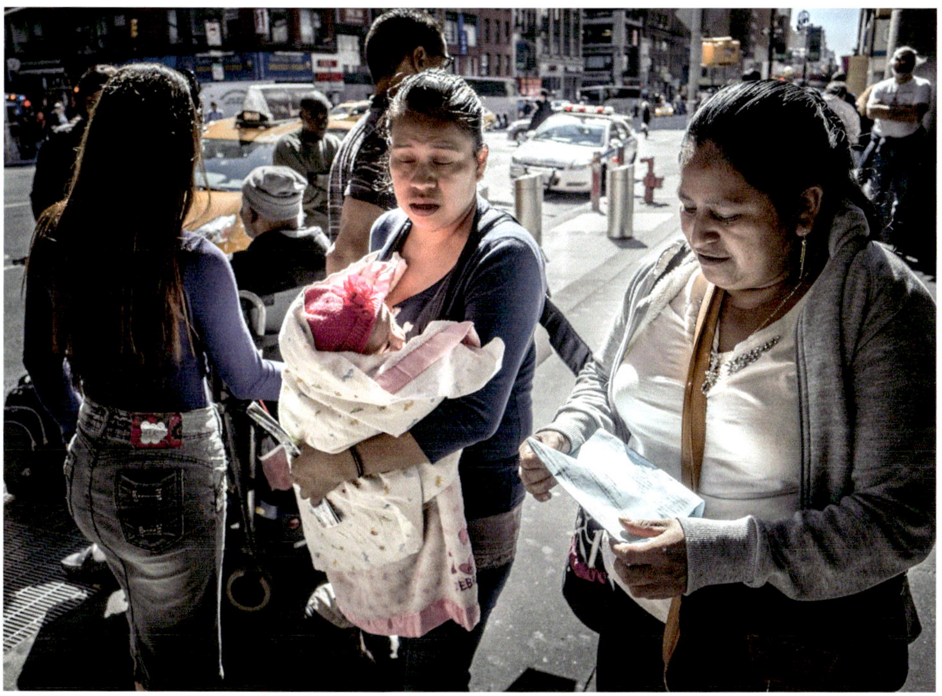

Mother and child with grandmother outside a postnatal office.

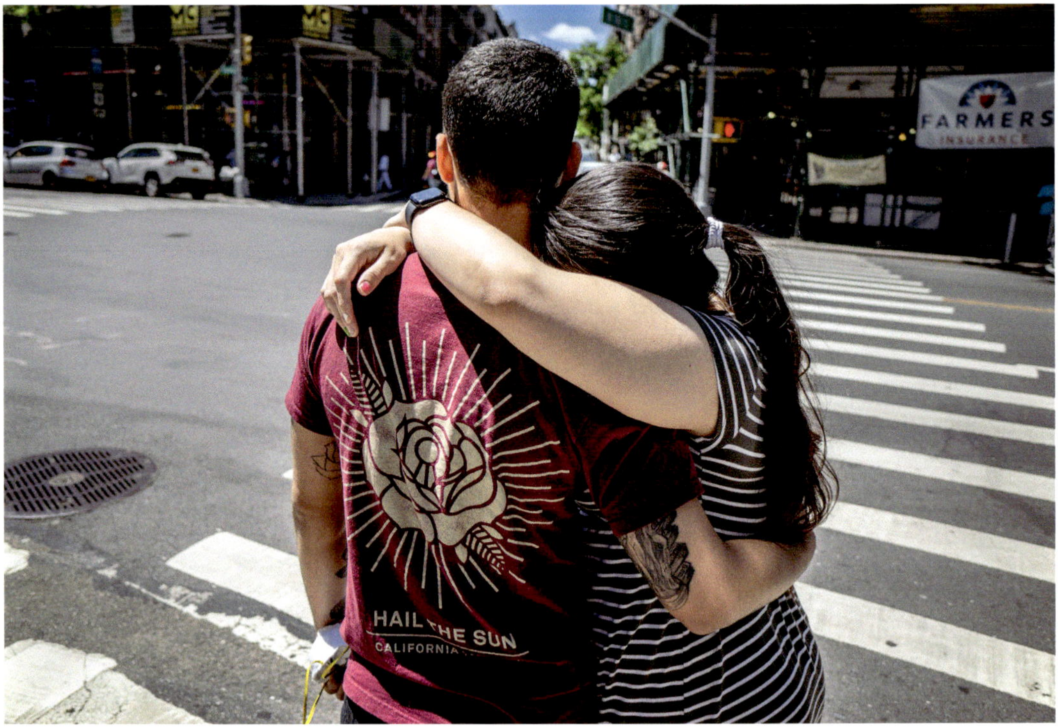

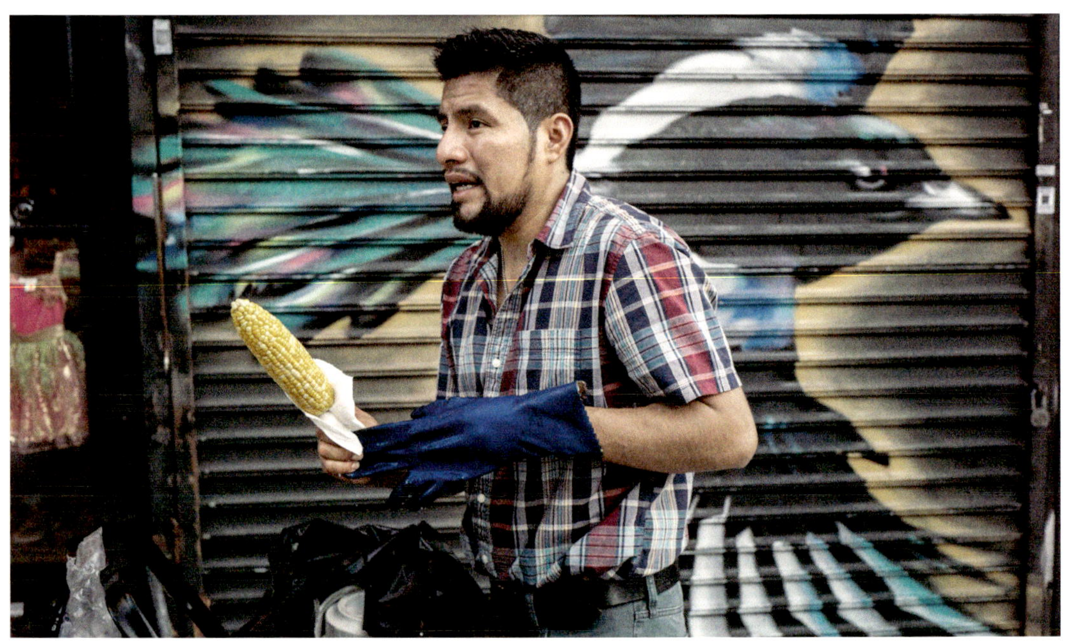

A couple embrace while waiting for the crosswalk light to change.

Standing in front of urban graffiti, a man removes his gloves to eat grilled corn.

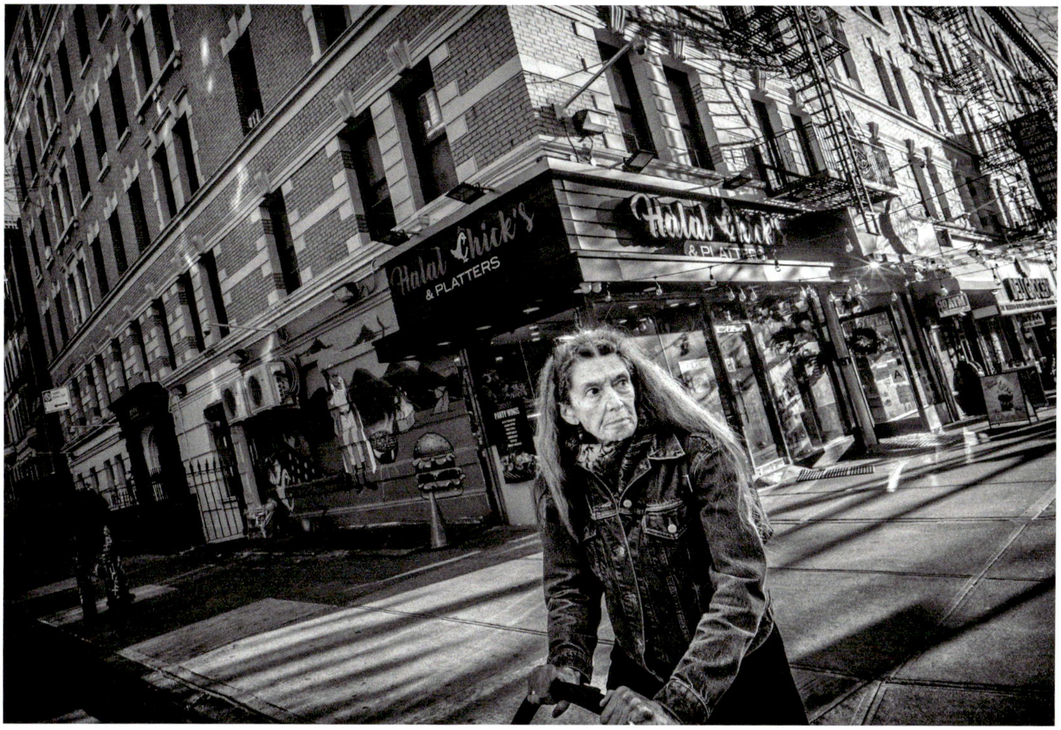

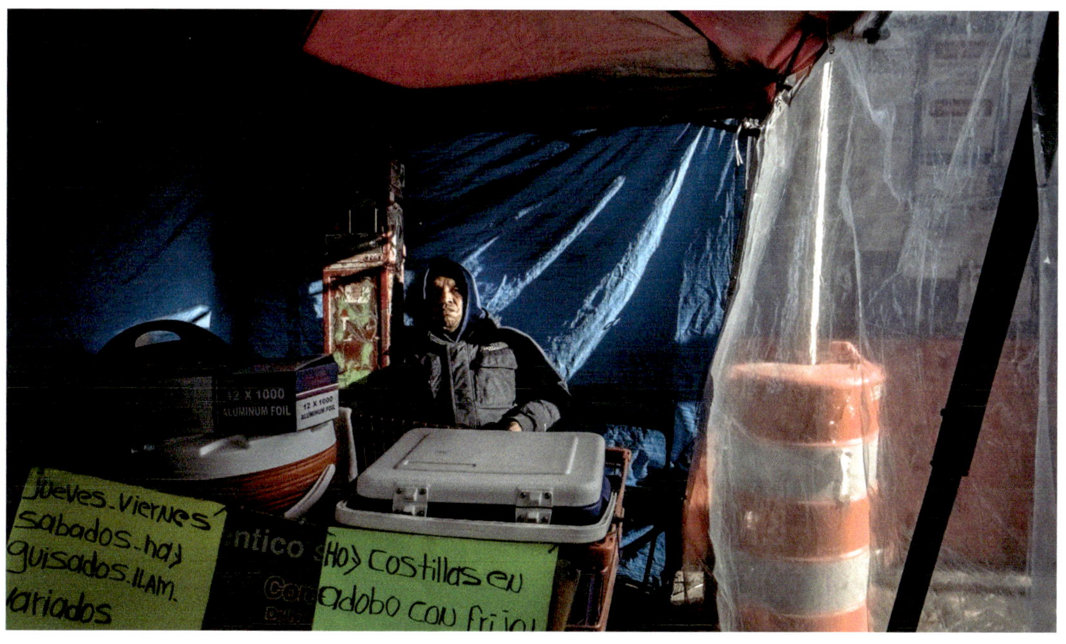

A woman pushes a cart down a sunlit Broadway, her gaze fixed on something in the distance.

Protected from the cold and wind by plastic sheeting, a Mexican food vendor waits for customers.

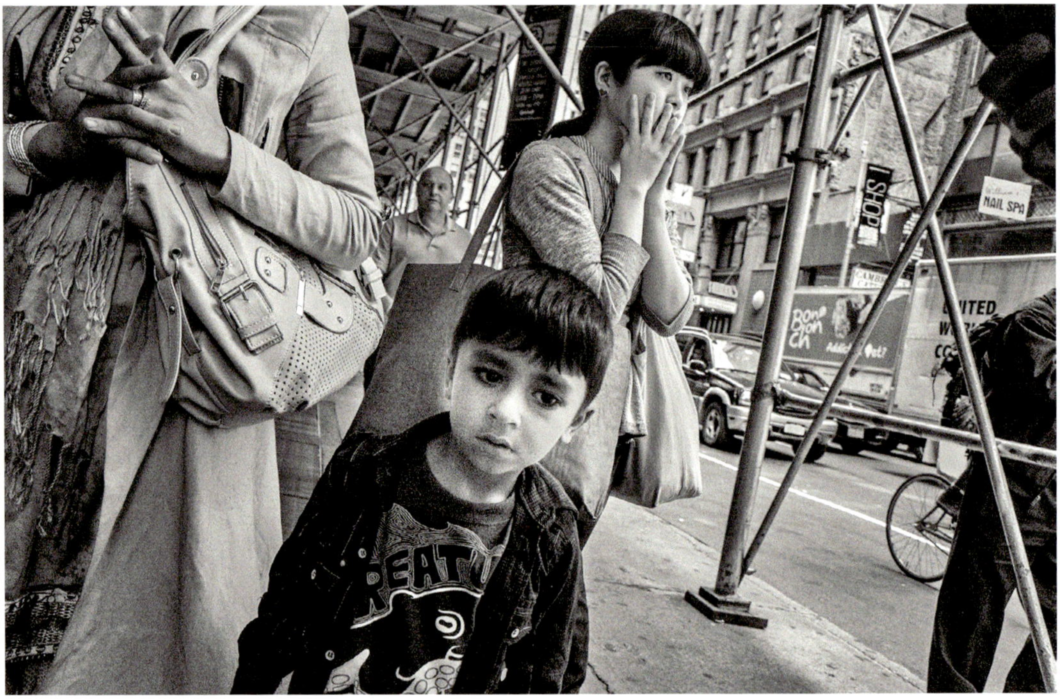

Children overwhelmed by the activity on the street.

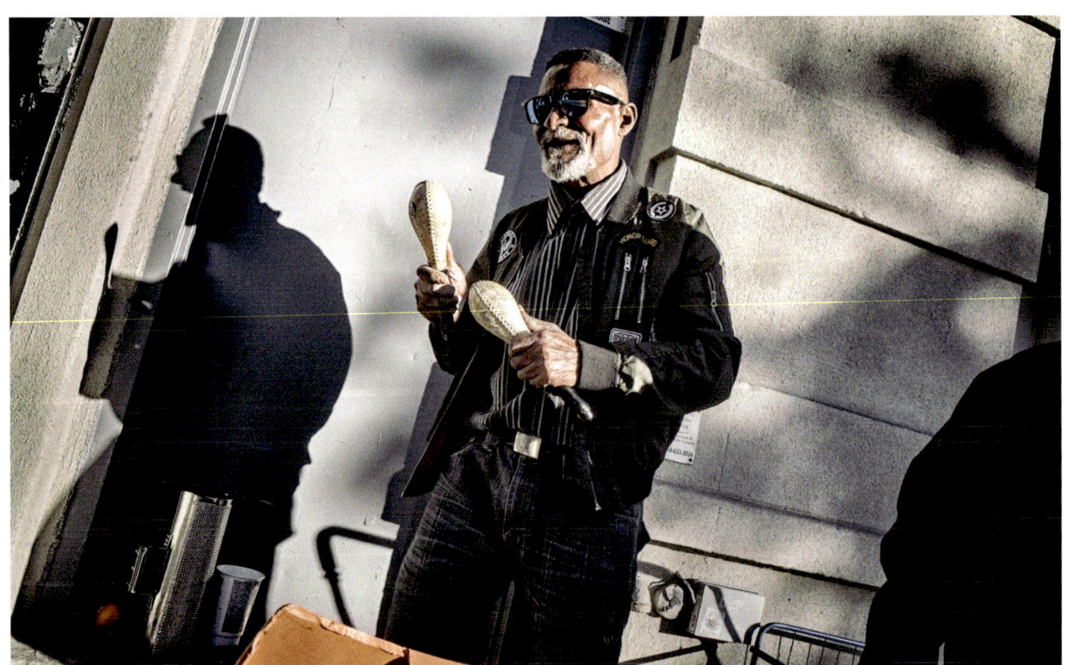

Playing maracas.

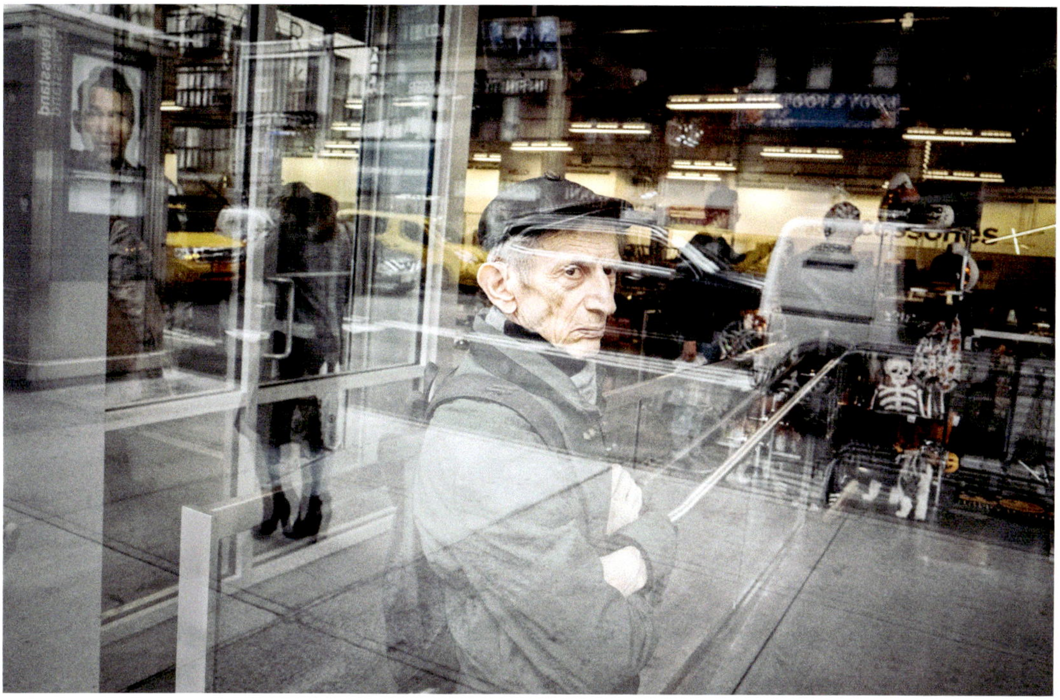

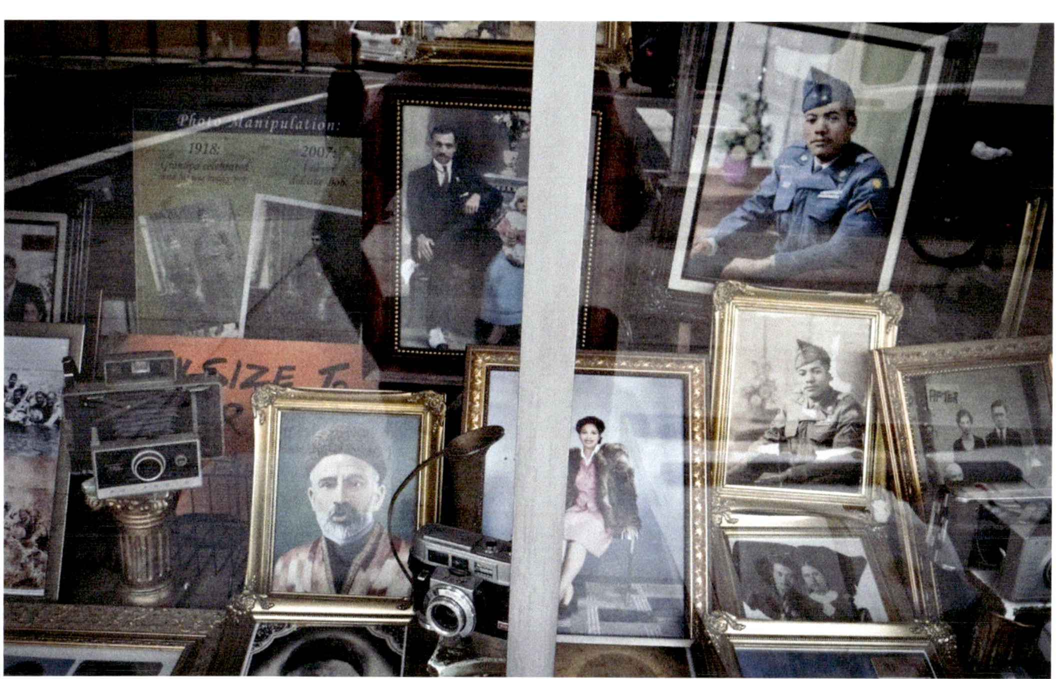

Looking through reflections of the street, a man peers through a coffee shop window.

The window display of a photo studio.

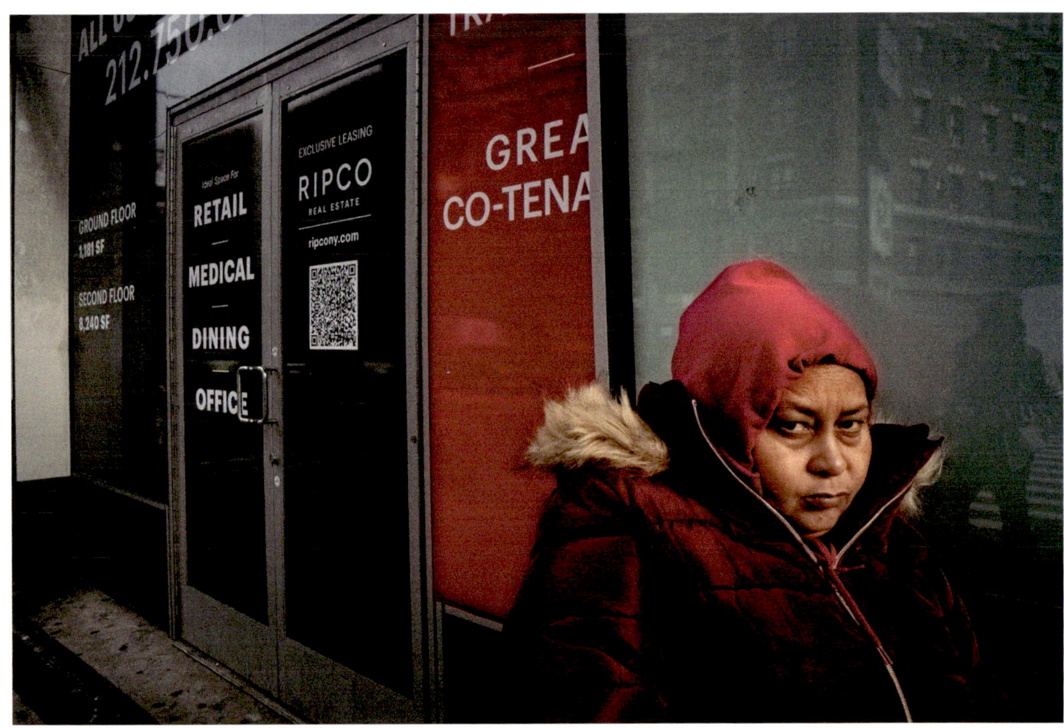

Under the George Washington Bridge Bus Terminal.

Opposite page: Santa Claus in a snow bubble.

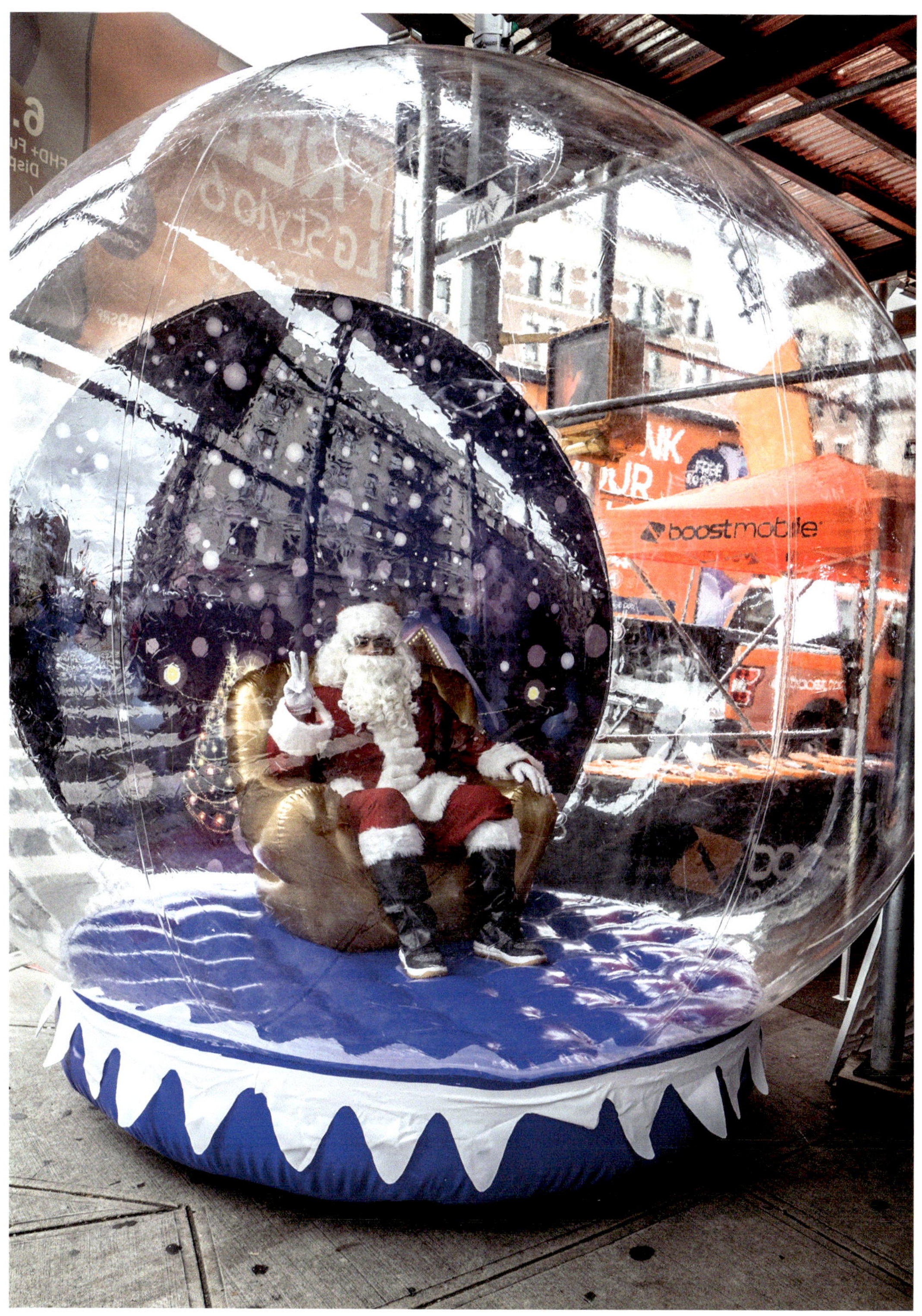
boost mobile

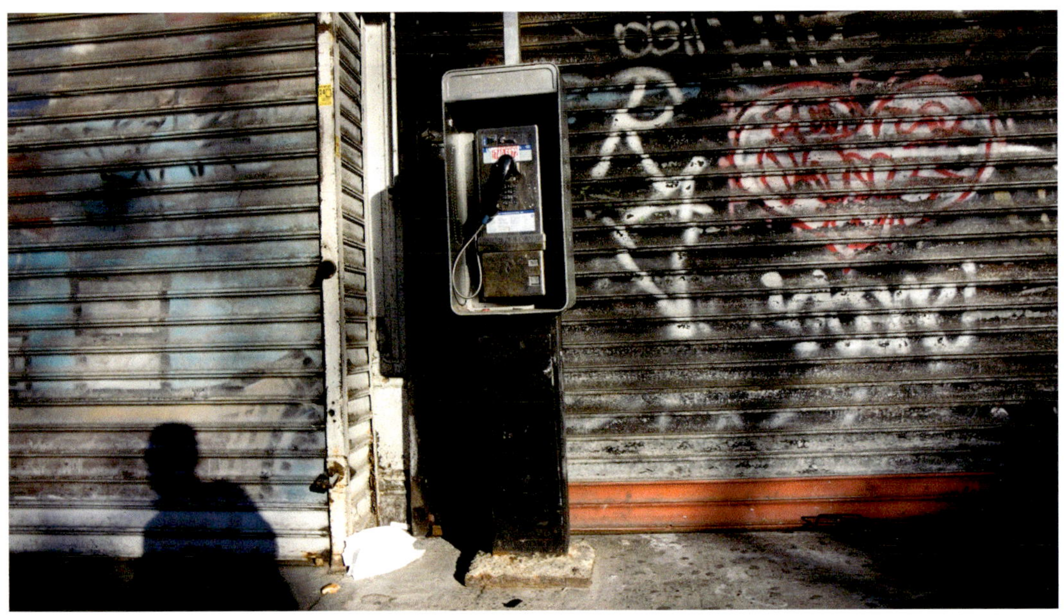

A lone payphone blends into its surroundings.

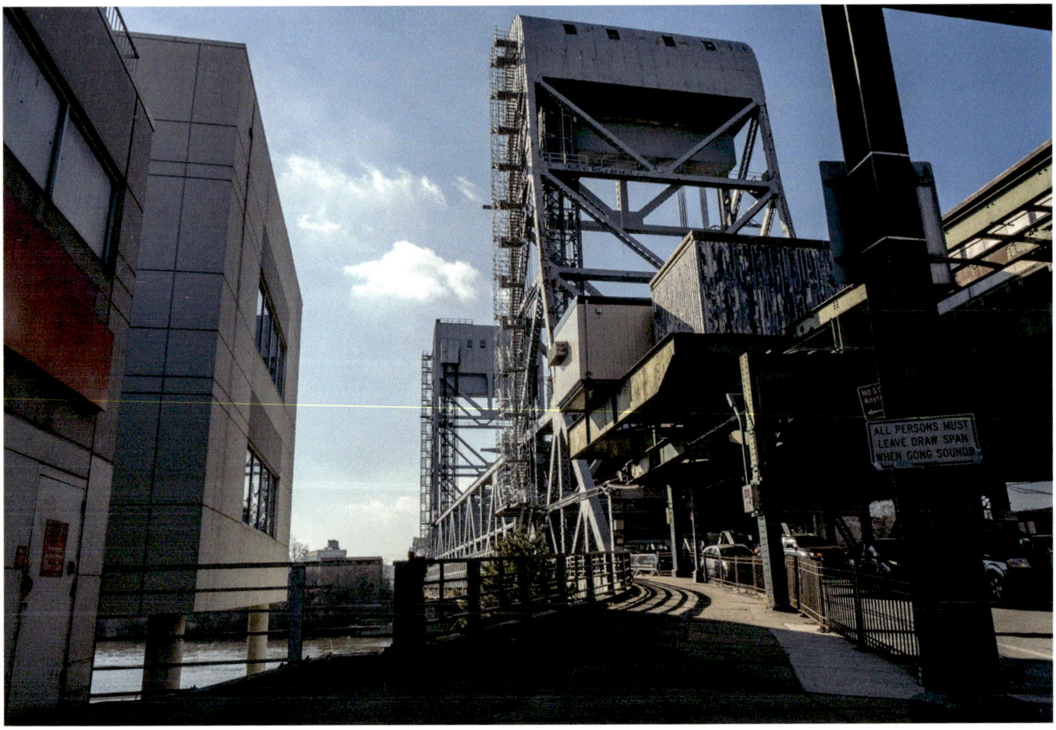

The Broadway Bridge spans the Harlem River from 220th Street and Broadway to 225th Street and Broadway. It connects northern Manhattan, Inwood, to the Bronx.